Good Housekeeping
Budget Cookbook

Contents

First published 1977 by
Octopus Books Limited
59 Grosvenor Street, London W1

© 1977 Octopus Books Limited

ISBN 0 7064 0597 8

Produced by Mandarin Publishers Limited
22a Westlands Road, Quarry Bay, Hong Kong

Printed in Hong Kong

Soups

heartwarming soups for all occasions

Cream of mushroom soup

serves 5-6

75 g (3 oz) butter
175 g (6 oz) onions, skinned and
    finely chopped
¼ kg (½ lb) button mushrooms,
    wiped and chopped
40 g (1½ oz) plain flour
900 ml (1½ pints) chicken stock,
    made from 2 stock cubes and
    900 ml (1½ pints) water
900 ml (1½ pints) milk
salt and freshly ground black
    pepper
¼ × 2.5 ml spoon (⅛ level tsp)
    garlic salt
the juice of half
    a lemon
fried croûtons

Melt the butter in a large pan and sauté the onions for 7 minutes, until soft but not coloured. Add the mushrooms, cover, and continue to cook for a further 5 minutes.

Stir in the flour and cook for 3 minutes, then slowly add the stock, stirring all the time. Bring to the boil and simmer gently for 20 minutes.

Add the milk and seasonings and lemon juice to taste. Simmer for a further 10 minutes. Do not boil after adding the milk. Garnish with croûtons of fried bread just before serving.

Cream of vegetable soup

serves 6

½ kg (1 lb) vegetables
50 g (2 oz) butter
400 ml (¾ pint) white stock
salt and pepper
25 g (1 oz) flour
600 ml (1 pint) milk

Wash and trim the chosen vegetable. Roughly slice (except peas). Melt 25 g (1 oz) butter in a pan, add the vegetable and fry gently for 5 minutes, without browning. Add the stock and simmer with the lid on for 10–15

minutes, until tender. Season to taste.

Meanwhile, make a white sauce, using 25 g (1 oz) butter, the flour and the milk. Sieve the soup and return to the pan with the white sauce, mix well, check the seasoning and reheat without boiling.

Note: *Suitable vegetables are onions, tomatoes, leeks, carrots, celery, or frozen peas. With onions or tomatoes, use only 150 ml (¼ pint) stock.*

Cream of celery soup

serves 4

25 g (1 oz) butter
1 head of celery, scrubbed and
    chopped
25 g (1 oz) flour
600 ml (1 pint) chicken stock
1 blade of mace
5 ml spoon (1 tsp) lemon juice
salt and freshly ground pepper
50 g (2 oz) carrot, peeled and finely
    diced
300 ml (½ pint) milk

Melt the butter, add the celery and fry gently for 5 minutes. Stir

Warming Cream of vegetable soup, made here with carrots

in the flour, cook for a few minutes, then gradually add the stock, stirring.

Add the mace and lemon juice, season with salt and pepper; bring to the boil, cover and simmer for 20 minutes. Discard the mace.

Purée the soup in a blender or work through a sieve, return it to the pan, add the diced carrot and simmer until the garnish is tender – about 15 minutes. Remove from the heat, add the milk and adjust the seasoning if necessary.

Cream of celery and tomato soup

serves 6

75 g (3 oz) butter
175 g (6 oz) onions, skinned and
    sliced
¾ kg (1½ lb) celery, scrubbed and
    sliced
¾ kg (1½ lb) tomatoes, skinned
    and sliced
1.1 litre (2 pints) chicken stock
2.5 ml spoon (½ level tsp) sweet
    basil
salt and freshly ground black
    pepper
50 g (2 oz) flour

600 ml (1 pint) milk
chopped parsley

Fry the onions gently in 50 g (2 oz) butter in a large pan, for 5 minutes. Add the celery and cook for a further 5 minutes.

Add the tomatoes, chicken stock and basil, season well and bring to the boil. Reduce the heat, cover the pan and simmer for about 45 minutes.

Sieve, or purée in a blender.

Make a roux by melting the remaining butter in a clean pan and stirring in the flour. Cook over a low heat for 2–3 minutes, remove from the heat and add the milk slowly, stirring until well blended.

Gradually add the vegetable purée, bring to the boil, adjust seasoning and simmer for a further 15 minutes. Sprinkle on the chopped parsley just before serving.

Brown onion soup

serves 6

15 ml spoon (1 tbsp) cooking oil
25 g (1 oz) butter
½ kg (1 lb) onions, skinned and
    finely chopped
1 clove garlic, skinned and crushed
1 beef stock cube
900 ml (1½ pints) boiling water
salt and pepper

Heat the oil and butter in a large pan and fry the onion over gentle heat for about 20 minutes, until soft but not coloured. Add the garlic, dissolve the stock cube in the boiling water, add to the pan, cover and simmer for 30 minutes. Adjust seasoning.

Potato and onion soup

serves 4

50 g (2 oz) butter
¼ kg (½ lb) onions, skinned and
    thinly sliced
½ kg (1 lb) potatoes, peeled and
    diced
600 ml (1 pint) chicken stock
300 ml (½ pint) milk
salt and pepper

¼ kg (½ lb) tomatoes, skinned and
    seeded
25 g (1 oz) cheese, grated
15 ml spoon (1 level tbsp) chopped
    parsley

Melt the butter and fry the onions
for 10 minutes. Add the potatoes,
cover and continue to cook over a
low heat for a further 10 minutes.
Add the stock and cook until the
potatoes are soft and mushy. Add
the milk and sieve or purée in a
blender. Adjust the seasoning.
Slice the tomato flesh in strips
and add to the soup, together with
the cheese and parsley. Reheat
before serving.

French onion
soup

serves 4

50 g (2 oz) butter
sugar
½ kg (1 lb) onions, skinned and
    sliced
900 ml (1½ pints) brown stock
salt and pepper
50–75 g (2–3 oz) Cheddar cheese,
    grated
4 thin slices French bread, toasted
white wine (optional)

Melt the butter, add a few grains
of sugar and fry the onions slowly
until well browned and soft. Stir
in the stock, bring to the boil and
simmer, with the lid on, for 30
minutes. Season to taste.
Pour into flameproof soup bowls.
Sprinkle the grated cheese on the
slices of French bread and float
one in each bowl of soup. Place
the bowls under a hot grill or in
the oven at 230°C (450°F) mark 8
until the cheese melts and bubbles, then serve immediately,
with more grated cheese if
required. A dash of dry white
wine may be added to the soup
just before pouring into the
bowls, if wished.

Celery soup

serves 4-6

1 large head of celery, scrubbed
25 g (1 oz) butter
2 medium-sized onions, skinned
    and finely chopped

Use your own homemade brown stock in French onion soup for a more concentrated flavour

600 ml (1 pint) chicken stock or 1
    chicken stock cube dissolved in
    600 ml (1 pint) boiling water
salt and freshly ground black
    pepper
1 bay leaf
300 ml (½ pint) milk
2 × 15 ml spoons (2 level tbsps)
    cornflour
150 ml (¼ pint) single cream

Chop the celery stalks, reserving
a few of the leaves for decoration.
Melt the butter in a large sauce
pan. Fry the celery and onion
gently for 2 minutes and then add
the stock and seasonings. Cover
and bring to simmering point.
Cook for 30 minutes. Remove the
bay leaf.
Purée in a blender or work
through a coarse sieve and return
to the heat in a clean saucepan.
Blend together the milk and the

cornflour and add to the saucepan. Bring to the boil, stirring all
the time. Remove the pan from
the heat and stir in the cream.
Adjust the seasoning if necessary.
Garnish with celery leaves.

Broad bean
soup

serves 3-4

50 g (2 oz) butter
100 g (4 oz) chopped onion
1 clove garlic, skinned and crushed
25 g (1 oz) flour
600 ml (1 pint) chicken or ham
    stock
¼ kg (½ lb) shelled broad beans,
    fresh or frozen

5 ml spoon (1 level tsp) dried
    thyme
lemon juice
salt and pepper
flaked almonds for garnish
    (optional)

Fry the onion and garlic in the
butter until soft but not coloured.
Stir in the flour, cook for 2
minutes and then add the stock.
Bring to the boil and add the
broad beans and thyme; simmer,
covered, until the beans are tender. Blend or sieve the contents of
the pan, adding more stock if
necessary to give a thin creamy
consistency.
Adjust the seasoning with lemon
juice, salt and pepper. If wished,
sauté a few flaked almonds in butter and add to the soup just before
reheating.

Chilled cucumber soup

serves 4

1 small onion, skinned and sliced
900 ml (1½ pints) white stock
1 large or 2 small cucumbers
sprig of mint
15 ml spoon (1 level tbsp)
  cornflour
2–3 × 15 ml spoons (2–3 tbsps)
  single cream
salt and pepper
green colouring

Simmer the onion for 15 minutes in a pan with the stock. Peel and chop the cucumber (saving a little for garnish), and add to the stock with the mint; simmer for about 10 minutes, or until the cucumber is cooked. Sieve the soup or purée in an electric blender, return it to the pan and reheat. Blend the cornflour with a little cold water to a smooth cream. Stir in a little of the hot soup, return the mixture to the pan and bring to the boil, stirring until it thickens. Cook for a further 2–3 minutes. Stir in the cream and season to taste.
Tint the soup delicately with green colouring, pour it into a large bowl, cover and chill. Serve with 2 or 3 slices of cucumber floating on top of the soup and serve cheese straws as an accompaniment.

Oxtail soup

serves 3-4

½ oxtail, jointed
15 g (½ oz) butter or margarine
1 onion, skinned and chopped
1 small carrot, peeled and sliced
1 celery stalk, scrubbed and sliced
1 litre (1¾ pints) brown stock
50 g (2 oz) lean ham or bacon,
  chopped
bouquet garni
salt and pepper
25 g (1 oz) flour
squeeze lemon juice

Wash and dry the oxtail and trim off any excess fat. Fry the pieces of oxtail in the fat with the vegetables for 5 minutes, until evenly

Chilled cucumber soup makes a good start to a warm evening

browned. Just cover with the stock and bring to the boil. Add the chopped ham or bacon, bouquet garni and seasoning, cover the saucepan and simmer for 3–4 hours, until the tail meat is tender. As oxtail is very fatty, it is necessary to skim the soup occasionally with a metal spoon. Strain the soup, remove the meat from the bones and cut the meat up neatly.
Return the meat and strained liquor to the pan and reheat. Blend the flour and a little water to a smooth cream. Stir in a little of the hot liquid and return the mixture to the pan. Bring to the boil, stirring until it thickens, and cook for about 5 minutes. Add a squeeze of lemon juice and seasoning to taste before serving.

Watercress soup

serves 6

For savoury butter:
25 g (1 oz) butter

paprika
chopped chives

100 g (4 oz) butter
50 g (2 oz) plain flour
700 ml (1¼ pints) chicken or veal
  stock
300 ml (½ pint) milk
salt and freshly ground black
  pepper
75 g (3 oz) onions, skinned and
  chopped
2 bunches watercress

Beat together 25 g (1 oz) butter, a little paprika and a few chopped chives. Roll out between sheets of non-stick paper. Chill.
Melt 75 g (3 oz) butter in a pan and stir in the flour. Cook over gentle heat for 1–2 minutes. Remove from the heat and stir in all the stock and milk. Return to the heat and bring to the boil, stirring continuously. Simmer gently for 3 minutes; season well. Sauté the onion in the remaining 25 g (1 oz) butter until soft. Wash the watercress and trim, leaving some of the stem. Chop roughly and add to the onion. Cover and cook for a further 4 minutes. Stir the sautéed vegetables into the soup and purée in a blender or

pass through a sieve. Gently reheat, season again and ladle into preheated bowls. Stamp the butter into fancy shapes, using small decorative cutters, and float 1 pat in each bowl of soup. Serve with pretzels.

Soupe à la paysanne

serves 6

50 g (2 oz) carrot
25 g (1 oz) turnip
25 g (1 oz) celery
50 g (2 oz) leek
25 g (1 oz) butter
salt and pepper
1.1 litre (2 pints) brown stock
bouquet garni, consisting of 3
  parsley stalks, bay leaf, sprig of
  thyme
croûtons

Cut the carrot and turnip into rough squares; thinly slice the celery and leeks. Bring a pan of water to the boil, add the vegetables and blanch for 3 minutes. Refresh under cold running water. Drain. Melt butter in a pan, add the vegetables and cook without colouring until tender. Pour the stock over them, bring to the boil, skim and add the bouquet garni. Cover and simmer for 20–30 minutes. Remove bouquet garni and skim well, using absorbent kitchen paper to remove any remaining fat. Adjust the seasoning if necessary.
Pour into a pre-heated tureen and serve the croûtons separately.

Minestrone alla Milanese

serves 4

3 potatoes, peeled and diced
½ small cabbage heart, washed
  and shredded
1 celery stalk, scrubbed and
  chopped
1 onion, skinned and chopped
1 clove garlic, skinned and
  chopped
3 tomatoes, skinned and roughly
  chopped
50 g (2 oz) shelled green peas or
  beans

Bortsch – Russian beetroot soup – served with a swirl of sour cream

Serve with grated Parmesan cheese in a separate dish, to be sprinkled on each individual serving.

Bortsch

serves 6

6 small raw beetroots (approx. 1 kg (2 lb)), peeled
2 medium-sized onions, skinned and chopped
2.3 litre (4 pints) seasoned beef stock
2 × 15 ml spoons (2 tbsps) lemon juice
6 × 15 ml spoons (6tbsps) dry sherry

Grate the beetroots coarsely and put it, together with the onions, in a pan with the stock. Bring to the boil and simmer without a lid for 45 minutes. Strain. Allow to cool then put in refrigerator to chill. Just before serving, add the lemon juice and sherry.

Consommé

serves 6

2 × 425 g (2 × 15 oz) cans consommé
salt and lemon juice

Heat consommé gently and add salt and lemon juice to taste.

Cock-a-leekie

serves 4

1 × 2½ kg (5 lb) boiling fowl or chicken
1.1 litre (2 pints) stock or water
4 leeks, cleaned and sliced
salt and pepper

Cover the fowl with stock or water, add the leeks and season-

4 × 15 ml spoons (4 tbsps) vegetable oil
2 rashers green streaky bacon, rinded and diced
1.7 litre (3 pints) stock or water
50 g (2 oz) long grain rice
100 g (4 oz) dried beans, soaked and cooked
salt and pepper
grated Parmesan cheese, for serving

Prepare the vegetables and cut them up fairly finely. Heat the oil in a large pan, fry the bacon and then sauté all the vegetables. Add the stock or water and bring to the boil.
When the liquid is boiling, add the rice and simmer for about 15–20 minutes. Add the dried beans and cook for a further 10 minutes. Season to taste.

Traditionally, boiling fowl is used to make Cock-a-leekie

ing and bring to the boil. Simmer gently for about 3½ hours, until tender.

Remove the chicken from the stock, carve off the meat and cut into fairly large pieces. Serve the soup with the chicken pieces in it or serve the soup on its own, with the chicken as a main course.

Mama's leek soup

serves 3-4

¼ kg (½ lb) leeks
50 g (2 oz) butter
300 ml–25 g (½ pint–1 oz) pkt. white sauce mix
600 ml (1 pint) milk
25 g (1 oz) Cheddar cheese, grated
salt and pepper
croûtons

Thinly slice the leeks, wash thoroughly and drain well. Melt the butter, add the leeks, cover and cook gently for about 10 minutes, until tender. Off the heat, shower in the contents of the sauce mix packet and gradually add the milk, stirring briskly. Bring to the boil, stirring, and cook for about 3 minutes. Purée in a blender or work through a wire sieve. Add the cheese, reheat and adjust seasoning – add a little more milk if necessary. Serve with croûtons.

Appetizer soup

serves 4

700 ml (1¼ pints) water
1 beef stock cube
1 chicken stock cube
425 g (15 oz) can tomatoes
1 medium onion, skinned and chopped
100 g (4 oz) carrots, peeled and thinly sliced
2 celery stalks, scrubbed and cut into 1 cm (½ in) lengths
3 peppercorns
½ × 2.5 ml spoon (¼ level tsp) dried sage
salt and freshly ground black pepper
grated Parmesan cheese to garnish

Put the water into a saucepan, then add the stock cubes, tomatoes, onion, carrot, celery, peppercorns and sage. Mix well, bring to the boil, cover and simmer gently for 1 hour. Adjust seasoning. Pour into individual soup bowls and sprinkle each with the Parmesan before serving.

Susan's German soup

serves 4

This soup is a meal in itself.

1.1 litre (2 pints) household stock
¼ kg (½ lb) potatoes, peeled
2 leeks, cleaned and sliced
¼ kg (½ lb) turnips, peeled and cubed
100 g (¼ lb) carrots, peeled and sliced
1 red or green pepper, sliced
2 celery stalks, sliced
¼ kg (½ lb) piece streaky bacon, rinded
¼ kg (½ lb) Cervelat or any salami without garlic e.g. German

Place the stock in a large pan with the potatoes cut in small pieces. Simmer until the potatoes are tender. Sieve potatoes and stock together or purée in a blender and return to the pan. Add leeks, turnips, carrots, pepper, celery and bacon and simmer gently, covered, for 1½–1¾ hours.
Meanwhile remove the skin from the Cervelat and cut into oblique slices. Add to the soup and simmer for a further 15 minutes. Adjust seasoning if necessary and cut the bacon into bite-size pieces before serving.

Kottosoupa

serves 6

50 g (2 oz) long grain rice
1.1 litre (2 pints) chicken stock
2 egg yolks, well beaten
juice of 1 lemon

Cook the rice in boiling salted water until tender, drain and add to the hot chicken stock. Simmer

gently for a few minutes, then bring almost to boiling point, remove from heat and whisk in egg yolks. Just before serving add the strained lemon juice.

Erwtensoep

serves about 6

¼ kg (½ lb) dried or split peas
1.7 litre (3 pints) water
¾ kg (1½ lb) meat (ham or boiling bacon for preference)
1 marrow bone, sawn into lengths
¼ kg (½ lb) potatoes, peeled and sliced
300 ml (½ pint) milk
salt and pepper
1 leek, washed, trimmed and cut into small pieces
1 celery stalk, scrubbed and cut into small pieces
chopped parsley

Wash the peas and soak them in 900 ml (1½ pints) of the water overnight.
The next day, simmer the meat and marrow bone in remaining 900 ml (1½ pints); after 1 hour, add the peas and the water in which they were soaked and cook until soft – about 1 hour. Add the potatoes after about 40 minutes. Take out the marrow bone and meat, scrape out the marrow and put this back into the soup. Keep the meat hot separately. Sieve or mash the soup thoroughly or purée it in a blender and add sufficient milk to thin. Season, add the leek and celery and cook for about 20 minutes, stirring occasionally. Stir in the parsley. Serve the soup in large bowls, with the chopped meat on separate plates.

Right: *Erwtensoep – a good, wholesome meal in itself*

Appetizers

clever ideas to whet your appetite

Tomato jelly rings

serves 4

½ kg (1 lb) firm, ripe tomatoes
2 small onions
1 small clove of garlic
5 ml spoon (1 level tsp) sugar
2.5 ml spoon (½ level tsp) salt
pinch of celery salt
pinch of grated nutmeg
1 bay leaf
5 ml spoon (1 level tsp)
 peppercorns
15 ml spoon (1 level tbsp)
 powdered gelatine
15 ml spoon (1 tbsp) tarragon
 vinegar
3 × 15 ml spoons (3 tbsps) lemon
 juice
watercress

Scald the tomatoes, remove the skins, cut in quarters and remove the centres if tough. Chop the onions and crush the garlic. Put the tomatoes, onions, garlic, sugar, salts and nutmeg in a pan, add the bay leaf and peppercorns tied in muslin, and cook over a low heat until the onion is tender. Remove the muslin bag.
Dissolve the gelatine in 2 × 15 ml spoons (2 tbsps) water in a small basin over hot water. Work the tomato mixture in an electric blender, rub it through a sieve and turn into a measure. Add the vinegar and lemon juice and if necessary make up to 600 ml (1 pint) with water. Add the dissolved gelatine, pour into wetted individual ring moulds and leave to set.
To serve, turn out moulds and garnish with watercress.

Glazed onions with sultanas

serves 4·6

½ kg (1 lb) pickling onions
4 × 15 ml spoons (4 tbsps) dry
 white wine
175 ml (6 fl oz) water
2 × 15 ml spoons (2 tbsps) lemon
 juice
2 × 15 ml spoons (2 tbsps) sultanas
2 × 10 ml spoons (4 level tsps)
 sugar
2 × 15 ml spoons (2 level tbsps)
 tomato paste
pinch of thyme
salt
freshly ground pepper
2 × 10 ml spoons (4 tsps) salad oil
chopped parsley for garnish

Dip onions in boiling water, drain and skin them. Place in a saucepan with all remaining ingredients except the salad oil and parsley. Bring to the boil, reduce heat, cover and simmer gently for about 30 minutes until tender but still crisp.
Increase the heat and boil rapidly in an open pan until the sauce becomes syrupy.
Chill onions. Just before serving stir in the salad oil. Garnish with parsley.

Cucumber portugaise

serves 6

2 large cucumbers (or 4 small
 ridge cucumbers)
4 × 15 ml spoons (4 tbsps) cooking
 oil
100 g (4 oz) onion, skinned and
 finely chopped
4 firm, ripe tomatoes, skinned and
 seeded
10 ml spoon (2 level tsps) tomato
 paste
2 × 15 ml spoons (2 tbsps) garlic
 vinegar
pinch of dried thyme
salt and freshly ground black
 pepper

Thinly pare the cucumbers using a potato peeler, then cut into 2.5 cm (1 in) lengths. Cut each piece into quarters along the length. Remove the centre seeds with the point of a knife and discard. Plunge into boiling salted water for 5 minutes; drain and refresh under cold running water. Sauté the onion in the oil until tender. Then, add the diced tomatoes, tomato paste, vinegar and thyme. Blend the cucumber with the tomato. Season well and turn into a serving dish. Chill thoroughly. Serve with crusty bread.

Florida cocktail

serves 6

3 large juicy grapefruit
6 oranges
caster sugar

Cut the grapefruit in half across the centre and divide them into segments using a small sharp knife or a grapefruit knife.
Divide the pieces between 6 small sundae glasses, pouring any juice over.
Peel the oranges, removing all the white pith and again divide into segments, add to the grapefruit in the glasses, with their juice. Dust with caster sugar and serve chilled.

Grapefruit and orange cocktail

serves 4

For mint freeze:
15 ml spoon (1 tbsp) lemon juice
240 ml (8½ fl oz) low calorie
 lemonade
2 × 15 ml spoons (2 tbsps) finely
 chopped fresh mint

2 large grapefruit
2 oranges

Mix together the lemon juice, lemonade and mint and pour into an ice tray. Freeze until soft ice, but not solid.
Meanwhile halve the grapefruit, using a zig-zag cut to give a decorative edge. Remove the flesh from the halves. Peel and segment the oranges, remove the membranes and cut into pieces. Mix with the grapefruit, pile into the grapefruit shells and top with the mint freeze.

Country pâté

serves 6

25 g (1 oz) butter
100 g (4 oz) onion, skinned and
 roughly chopped
100 g (4 oz) lean bacon, rinded and
 chopped
100 g (4 oz) belly of pork, rinded
 and cut into strips
175 g (6 oz) pig's liver, diced
175 g (6 oz) stewing steak, diced
100 g (4 oz) pie veal, diced
2 cloves garlic, crushed
75 ml (3 fl oz) red wine
2 × 15 ml spoons (2 tbsps) brandy
 or port
1 bay leaf
salt and black pepper
dash of Worcestershire sauce
bacon fat
½ beaten egg

Melt the butter in a large saucepan and fry the onion and bacon until they are light golden brown. Add the rest of the ingredients, except the egg, and bring to the boil. Cover the pan and simmer for 30 minutes.
Strain off the liquor and put the mixture through the mincer

Tomato jelly rings make an impressive – but cheap – first course

twice, using the finest blade. Mix thoroughly with the strained liquor and the beaten egg. Season again if necessary. Place in a foil-lined, lightly buttered 450 g (1 lb) loaf tin. Place in a roasting tin with water half way up and cook in the oven at 180°C (350°F) mark 4 for 1½ hours.

Remove from the oven and cool. Chill for at least 12 hours before turning out and serving.

Smoked fish pâté

serves 6

*200 g (7 oz) can smoked codling
  fillets
175 g (6 oz) butter
2.5 ml spoon (½ level tsp) cayenne
  pepper
2 × 15 ml spoons (2 level tbsps)
  chopped capers
2 × 15 ml spoons (2 level tbsps)
  chopped parsley
15 ml spoon (1 tbsp) lemon juice
salt and freshly ground black
  pepper
pinch of ground nutmeg
25 g (1 oz) butter, melted
cucumber slices to garnish*

Cook the codling fillets as directed. Drain, then remove any skin and flake the flesh. Cream the butter well, adding the cayenne by degrees to taste. Beat in the fish, capers, parsley and lemon juice. Season to taste. Spoon the pâté mixture either into one 15 cm (6 in) soufflé dish or into small individual dishes. Top with a little melted butter and chill. Garnish with cucumber slices.

A really refreshing start to a meal – Frozen pineapple cocktail

Fresh cod roe can also be used to make Cod roe pâté

Cod roe pâté

serves 6

*1 thin slice white bread
¼ kg (½ lb) can cod roe
1 small potato, peeled and boiled
1 clove garlic, skinned and crushed
few sprigs of parsley
juice of ½ lemon
5 ml spoon (1 tsp) cooking oil
salt and pepper
black olives, cucumber slices and
  lemon slices to garnish*

Crumb bread. Beat cod roe until smooth. Beat in breadcrumbs, potato, garlic, parsley and lemon juice. Add the oil, a few drops at a time, and when well blended, season to taste. Spoon into a shallow dish and garnish with olives, cucumber and lemon slices. Serve with crisp lettuce, gherkins and extra olives, Melba toast or hot toast fingers.

Frozen pineapple cocktail

serves 6

*450 g (16 oz) can crushed
  pineapple
300 ml (½ pint) unsweetened
  orange juice
300 ml (½ pint) unsweetened
  grapefruit juice
150 ml (¼ pint) low calorie ginger
  ale
2–3 drops liquid sweetener
mint sprigs for garnish*

Mix together all the ingredients except the mint. Pour into an ice-cube tray and freeze.
When frozen, but not solid, spoon into stemmed glasses and garnish with the mint.

Potted beef

serves 6

*½ kg (1 lb) stewing steak, cut into
  1 cm (½ in) cubes
150 ml (¼ pint) stock
1 clove
1 blade of mace
salt and pepper
50 g (2 oz) butter, melted
fresh bay leaves for garnish*

Put the meat in a casserole with the stock and seasonings. Cover and cook in the centre of the oven

at 180°C (350°F) mark 4 for 2½–3 hours, until tender. Remove the clove and mace and drain off the stock, setting it aside.
Mince the meat twice or place it in a blender and blend for several minutes until smooth. Add 25 g (1 oz) melted butter and enough of the reserved stock to moisten. Press into ramekins or soufflé dishes, cover with the remainder of the melted butter and chill. Serve garnished with a fresh bay leaf on each portion.

Anchovy toasts

serves 4

*2 slices bread
15 g (½ oz) butter
squeeze of lemon juice
5 canned anchovy fillets, chopped
pepper
pinch of ground nutmeg
pinch of ground mace
parsley*

Toast the bread and cut it into fingers. Melt the butter, add a squeeze of lemon juice, the anchovies, pepper, nutmeg and mace. Beat well and rub through a sieve. Spread this mixture on the fingers of hot toast and garnish with sprigs of parsley.
Similar savouries can be made with sardines or herrings.

Soft roe savoury

serves 4

*12 herring roes
butter for frying
4 slices of bread
salt and pepper
a squeeze of lemon juice
parsley*

Wash the roes, dry them well and fry gently in a small pan in some butter for 8–10 minutes until golden. Remove them from the pan, wipe out the pan with kitchen paper, heat a little more butter and fry the bread slices for 2–3 minutes until golden. Place the cooked roes on the fried bread, season, add a squeeze of lemon juice and garnish with a sprig of parsley.

Thrifty pâté

serves 6

575 g (1¼ lb) lean belly pork
¼ kg (½ lb) pig's or ox liver
100 g (4 oz) lean streaky bacon, rinded
100 g (4 oz) onion, chopped
1 small clove garlic, skinned
5 ml spoon (1 level tsp) salt
freshly ground black pepper
25 g (1 oz) butter

Remove the rind and any bones from the belly pork and dice. Rinse the liver under cold running water and dry on absorbent paper.

Cut into largish pieces. Mince the pork, liver, bacon, onion and garlic together three times. Work in the salt and pepper.

Turn into a 1.1 litre (2 pint) terrine or small casserole, cover and place in a small roasting tin with water half way up. Cook at 150°C (300°F) mark 2 for about 1½ hours. Remove the lid. Lay a double sheet of foil over the top, add weights and weigh down until quite cold, preferably in a refrigerator. Remove weights and covering. Scrape off excess fat. Melt butter over a low heat, pour over pâté and chill.

Serve Thrifty pâté with wafer-thin slices of toast

Fluffy cheese boats are good after dinner or with evening drinks

Potted cheese

100 g (4 oz) butter or margarine
pinch ground mace
½ × 2.5 ml spoon (¼ level tsp) dry mustard
2 × 15 ml spoons (2 tbsps) dry sherry
275 g (10 oz) Cheshire cheese, grated

Cream the butter or margarine, mace, mustard and sherry until really soft. Slowly beat in the cheese. Serve in small earthenware pots.
(This will keep for a fortnight in the refrigerator.)

Fluffy cheese boats

serves 4

For shortcrust pastry:
100 g (4 oz) flour
pinch of salt
25 g (1 oz) lard
25 g (1 oz) margarine
2 × 10 ml spoons (4 tsps) water (approx.)

For filling:
25 g (1 oz) butter or margarine
25 g (1 oz) flour
300 ml (½ pint) milk
100 g (4 oz) cheese, grated
salt and freshly ground black pepper
2 eggs, separated

Sift together the flour and the salt.

Cut the fat into small pieces, add to the flour and, using both hands, rub in with the finger tips until it resembles fine breadcrumbs. Add the water a little at a time, stirring with a round-bladed knife until the mixture begins to stick together. With 1 hand, collect it together and knead lightly to give a smooth, firm dough.

Wrap in greaseproof paper or polythene and chill for 15 minutes.

Roll out the pastry on a lightly floured board and use to line small boat-shaped moulds or patty tins. Bake blind near the top of the oven at 220°C (425°F) mark 7 for 15 minutes, or until cooked but still pale in colour.

Melt the fat, stir in the flour and cook for 2–3 minutes. Remove from the heat and gradually stir in the milk. Bring to the boil and continue to stir until the sauce thickens.

Remove from the heat and stir in 75 g (3 oz) cheese, the seasoning and egg yolks; pour into the pastry cases. Whisk the egg whites stiffly, spoon a little on to the top of each boat and sprinkle with the remaining cheese. Reduce the oven temperature to 180°C (350°F) mark 4 and return the cases to the oven for about 10 minutes, or until the filling is heated through and the topping is golden. Serve at once.

Meat

how to cook succulent meat dishes perfectly

Beef and pepper casserole

serves 6

1 kg (2 lb) chuck steak
2 × 15 ml spoons (2 tbsps) fat or oil
2 large onions, skinned and sliced
2 green peppers, seeded and sliced
40 g (1½ oz) flour
900 ml (1½ pints) brown stock
2 × 15 ml spoons (2 tbsps) tomato paste
salt and freshly ground black pepper
bouquet garni

Cut the meat into 2.5 cm (1 in) cubes. Heat the fat or oil and fry the onions until golden brown; remove and place in a casserole. Reserve a few slices of pepper and fry the rest lightly. Add to the onions in the casserole. Brown the meat in the remaining fat, adding only a few pieces at a time to the pan, so that the fat remains really hot. When the meat is well browned, transfer to the casserole with the vegetables. Add the flour to the fat remaining in the frying pan, stir well and gradually stir in the stock and tomato paste. Bring to the boil, season and pour over the meat and vegetables in casserole. Add bouquet garni. Cover and cook in the centre of the oven at 180°C (350°F) mark 4 for 1–1½ hours; 20 minutes before serving add the reserved slices of pepper and return to the oven. Remove the bouquet garni before serving.

A heartwarming meal to come home to – Braised beef with sour cream and mushrooms

Braised beef with sour cream and mushrooms

serves 6

1¾ kg (3½ lb) thick flank beef, trimmed free of fat
400 g (14 oz) can plum tomatoes
2 beef stock cubes
225 g (½ lb) onions, skinned and quartered
225 g (½ lb) carrots, peeled and halved
½ kg (1 lb) button mushrooms, washed and stalks removed
50 g (2 oz) butter
300 ml (½ pint) sour cream
chopped parsley for garnish

Cut the lean meat into thin strips. Pour the tomatoes into a large, flameproof casserole and crumble in the stock cubes. Arrange the meat in the centre with the onions, carrots and mushroom stalks round the sides. Cover tightly, preferably with foil and a lid. Cook at 170°C (325°F) mark 3 for about 2 hours.
Remove the lid and gently turn the meat in the juice. Cover, reduce heat to 150°C (300°F) mark 2 and cook for a further hour, or until tender.
Slice the mushrooms. Melt the butter and fry the mushrooms. Discard vegetables except tomatoes from casserole. On top of cooker, add mushrooms to beef and stir in half the sour cream. Reheat carefully, without boiling. Adjust the seasoning, stir in the remaining sour cream and garnish with chopped parsley.

Beef curry

serves 6

1 kg (2 lb) best stewing steak
25 g (1 oz) seasoned flour
50 g (2 oz) butter
300 ml (½ pint) beef stock
5 ml spoon (1 tsp) tomato paste
salt and pepper
600 ml (1 pint) curry sauce

Trim the beef and cut into even-sized pieces. Toss in the seasoned flour, then fry in the melted butter until brown on all sides. Stir in the stock and tomato paste and add a little seasoning. Bring to the boil, then pour into a casserole. Cover and cook in the oven at 170°C (325°F) mark 3 for 2–2½ hours or until tender. Place meat in a saucepan and stir in curry sauce. Reheat gently.

Beef el dorado

serves 4

2 small onions, skinned
4 young carrots, pared
3 × 15 ml spoons (3 level tbsps) cooking oil
½ kg (1 lb) lean chuck steak, cubed
seasoned flour
300 ml (½ pint) light ale
3 × 2.5 ml spoons (1½ level tsps) black treacle
75 g (3 oz) sultanas
salt and pepper

Thickly slice the onions; cut the carrots into thin rings. Heat the oil and fry the onions and carrots for about 2 minutes; remove from the pan. Toss the meat in seasoned flour and fry it until lightly coloured. Return the vegetables

to the pan, pour in the light ale, bring to the boil and add the treacle and sultanas. Place in an ovenproof dish, cover and cook at 170°C (325°F) mark 3 for 2–2½ hours, or until tender. Check seasoning. Serve accompanied by natural yoghurt sprinkled with chopped parsley.

Burgerbraise

serves 4

100 g (4 oz) white bread
350 g (12 oz) lean chuck steak
1 onion, skinned and quartered
pinch of mixed herbs
salt and pepper
flour
25 g (1 oz) lard
400 g (14 oz) can tomatoes, made up to 300 ml (½ pint) with water

Make the bread into crumbs. Mince the meat and onion and add to the breadcrumbs with the herbs and seasonings. Mix well and shape into 4 round, flat cakes. Toss them in a little flour.
Melt the lard in a frying pan and fry the burgers until they are brown. Add the tomatoes, cover and simmer for 25-30 minutes, until thoroughly cooked.

Carbonnade of beef

serves 6

1½ kg (3 lb) lean stewing steak, cut into 1 cm (½ in) cubes
salt and pepper
75 g (3 oz) fat or oil
100 g (4 oz) lean bacon rashers, rinded and chopped
50 g (2 oz) plain flour
400 ml (¾ pint) beer
400 ml (¾ pint) stock or water
3 × 15 ml spoons (3 tbsps) vinegar
¾ kg (1½ lb) onions, skinned and chopped
2 cloves garlic, skinned and chopped
bouquet garni

Season the meat and fry a little at a time in the fat or oil until brown – about 5 minutes for each batch. Add the bacon and continue cooking for a few minutes. Remove any meat and bacon from the pan, stir in the flour and brown lightly. Gradually add the beer, stock and vinegar, stirring continuously until the mixture thickens. Fill a casserole with layers of meat, bacon, onion and garlic. Pour the sauce over and add the bouquet garni. Cover and cook at 150°C (300°F) mark 2 for

about 4 hours. Add a little more stock while cooking if the sauce seems very thick. Remove the bouquet garni before serving.

Hungarian goulash

serves 4

600 g (1¼ lb) chuck steak
seasoned flour
2 onions, skinned and chopped
1 green pepper, seeded and chopped
a little dripping
10 ml spoon (2 level tsps) tomato paste
salt and pepper
grated nutmeg
25 g (1 oz) flour
300 ml (½ pint) stock
2 large tomatoes, skinned and roughly chopped
bouquet garni
150 ml (¼ pint) beer
10 ml spoon (2 level tsps) paprika

Cut the beef into small pieces and coat with seasoned flour. Sauté the chopped onions and pepper lightly in a little dripping, then add the meat and fry lightly on all sides. Stir in the tomato paste, seasonings and flour. Add the stock, tomatoes and bouquet garni and simmer gently for 1 hour, then add the beer and paprika and cook for about a further 20 minutes, until fork tender. Remove the bouquet garni and serve.
Goulash is traditionally served with plain boiled potatoes.

Marinated steak pot

serves 6

1 kg (2 lb) chuck steak
2 × 15 ml spoons (2 tbsps) garlic vinegar
50 g (2 oz) dripping
40 g (1½ oz) flour
100 g (¼ lb) button onions, skinned
100 g (¼ lb) button mushrooms, wiped and stalks removed
100 g (¼ lb) streaky bacon, rinded and diced
600 ml (1 pint) beef stock
1 bay leaf

Serve classic Carbonnade of beef with chunks of crusty French bread and fresh butter

15 ml spoon (1 level tbsp) tomato
  paste
bouquet garni
chopped parsley

Cut the meat into neat pieces, put it in a polythene bag and add the vinegar. Toss the meat well, place the bag in a deep bowl and leave the meat overnight to marinate.

Melt the dripping in a frying pan. Drain the meat, reserving the juices, and coat with the flour. Fry it until sealed and brown on all sides. Remove the meat from the pan, add the onions, mushrooms and bacon and fry for 5 minutes. Place the mixture together with the meat and juices in a casserole.

Pour the stock into the frying pan, stir to loosen the sediment and add the bay leaf, tomato paste and bouquet garni. Bring to the boil and pour over the meat. Cover tightly and cook in the oven at 170°C (325°F) mark 3 for about 1½ hours. Discard the bay leaf and bouquet garni and serve sprinkled generously with chopped parsley.

Cheese and beef roly poly

serves 4-6

For suet crust:
225 g (8 oz) self-raising flour
100 g (4 oz) shredded suet
100 g (4 oz) Cheddar cheese, finely
  grated
pinch of salt
cold water to mix

For filling:
½ kg (1 lb) beef, minced
100 g (4 oz) onion, skinned and
  finely chopped
5 ml spoon (1 level tsp) dried
  marjoram
25 g (1 oz) fresh white
  breadcrumbs
salt and pepper
1 egg, beaten

Mix in a bowl the flour, suet, cheese and salt. Add enough cold water to mix to a soft elastic dough. Knead lightly on a floured board and roll into a rectangle 30 cm by 25 cm (12 in by 10 in). In a bowl mix together the beef, onion, marjoram, breadcrumbs,

salt and pepper. Add the egg and mix well. Spread the meat mixture over the rectangle of pastry to within 2.5 cm (1 in) of one long edge and brush the remaining strip with water. Carefully roll up and wrap loosely in oiled aluminium foil. Seal the ends well.

Place the roly poly in a roasting tin in 0.5 cm (¼ in) of water. Bake in the centre of the oven at 170°C (325°F) mark 3, for 2 hours. Serve hot.

Potato moussaka

serves 4

50 g (2 oz) margarine
1 large onion, skinned and finely
  chopped
½ kg (1 lb) cooked lamb, minced
1 clove garlic, skinned and crushed
1 beef stock cube, dissolved in
  150 ml (¼ pint) boiling water
15 ml spoon (1 level tbsp) tomato
  paste
2.5 ml spoon (½ level tsp) dried
  oregano
salt and pepper
50 g (2 oz) lard

¾ kg (1½ lb) potatoes, peeled and
  sliced
25 g (1 oz) flour
200 ml (7 fl oz) milk
pinch of ground nutmeg
1 egg yolk
25 g (1 oz) Cheddar cheese, grated
1 tomato, sliced

Melt 25 g (1 oz) margarine in a large pan, add the onion and fry for 5 minutes, until golden. Add the lamb and garlic, stir in the stock, tomato paste, oregano and season. Melt the lard in a large frying pan and fry the potato slices for about 10 minutes, or until golden. Drain off the fat. Melt the remaining margarine in a pan, stir in the flour and cook over gentle heat for 2 minutes. Remove the pan from the heat, stir in the milk gradually then bring to the boil, stirring. Cook for 2 minutes. Stir in the nutmeg and season to taste. Beat in the egg yolk.

Cover the base of a buttered casserole with a layer of potatoes, and season. Spread half the meat mixture over the potatoes; top with half the remaining potatoes and half the sauce. Finish with layers of potatoes, meat and sauce. Sprinkle the cheese over the top and bake in the centre of the oven at 190°C (375°F) mark 5 for 35 minutes. Garnish with tomatoes.

Potato moussaka makes a good, filling meal for hungry people

Steak and kidney pudding

serves 4

225 g (8 oz) suetcrust pastry i.e.
  225 g (8 oz) flour, etc.
100 g (¼ lb) kidney, skinned and
  cored
225–350 g (½–¾ lb) stewing steak,
  cut into 1 cm (½ in) cubes
2 × 15 ml spoons (2 level tbsps)
  seasoned flour
1 onion, skinned and chopped

Half-fill a steamer or large saucepan with water and put it on to boil. Grease a 900 ml (1½ pint) pudding basin. Cut off a quarter of the pastry to make the lid. Roll out the remainder and use to line the basin.

Slice the kidney and coat both the steak and the kidney with seasoned flour. Fill the basin with the meat, onion and 2–3 × 15 ml spoons (2–3 tbsps) of water.

Roll out the remainder of the pastry to a round the size of the basin top and damp the edge of it. Place on top of the meat and seal the edges of the pastry well.

Cover with greased greaseproof paper or foil and steam over rapidly boiling water for about 4 hours, refilling the pan as necessary with boiling water.

The meat can be prepared and stewed with the onion for about 2 hours earlier in the day or the previous night before being used for the filling. In this case, reduce the steaming time to 1½–2 hours.

Upside-down beef and potato pie

serves 4

75 g (3 oz) butter or margarine
100 g (4 oz) fresh white
  breadcrumbs
1 kg (2 lb) old potatoes, peeled
salt and pepper
1 large onion, skinned and
  chopped
1 clove garlic, skinned and crushed
6 gherkins, chopped

225 g (½ lb) button mushrooms, washed and sliced
½ kg (1 lb) lean beef, minced
15 ml spoon (1 level tbsp) mild curry powder
15 ml spoon (1 level tbsp) flour

Grease a 1.4 litre (2½–pint) oven-proof dish.
Heat 50 g (2 oz) fat in a frying pan, add the breadcrumbs and fry, stirring, until golden. Place in the greased dish. Boil the potatoes until just tender; drain, mash and season with salt and pepper. Heat the remaining butter and fry the onion until golden. Add the garlic, gherkins, mushrooms, beef and curry powder and fry for 10 minutes, stirring frequently. Add the flour and mix well.
Arrange half the potatoes over the crumbs in the dish. Cover with the meat mixture and remaining potatoes. Press well down.
Cook in the oven at 190°C (375°F) mark 5 for 1–1¼ hours. To serve, invert on to a serving dish and garnish with tomato and parsley.

West African beef curry

serves 4

1 kg (2 lb) chuck steak
25 g (1 oz) flour
large pinch of paprika
large pinch of cayenne pepper
large pinch of chilli powder
corn oil
225 g (½ lb) onions, skinned and chopped
15 ml spoon (1 level tbsp) desiccated coconut
2 × 15 ml spoons (2 level tbsps) curry powder
15 ml spoon (1 level tbsp) curry paste
1 small clove garlic, skinned and crushed
a few drops Tabasco sauce
600 ml (1 pint) stock

Trim the steak and cut it into serving-size pieces. Toss in the flour seasoned with the paprika, cayenne and chilli powder, using just enough flour to coat the steak thoroughly. Heat 5 x 5 ml spoons (1½ tbsps) oil in a large saucepan and fry the onions until evenly browned. Add the coconut, curry powder, curry paste, garlic, Tabasco and stock. Bring the mixture to the boil.

Fresh persimmon (top right) *are just one of the exotic fruits you can serve with West African beef curry*

In a large frying pan, heat enough oil to just cover the base and fry the meat a little at a time, until sealed and brown. Add the drained meat to the curry sauce, cover and simmer until the meat is tender – about 2 hours. Serve with sliced fruits and raw vegetables, desiccated coconut and poppadums.

Wiener beef braise

serves 6

¾ kg (1½ lb) buttock steak (thick flank or topside), cut into 12 thin slices
12 small frankfurters
75 g (3 oz) dripping
2 medium onions, skinned and chopped
4 carrots, peeled and cubed
1 large turnip, peeled and cubed
3 celery stalks, scrubbed and sliced
400 ml (¾ pint) beef stock, made with a cube
salt and pepper
¾ kg (1½ lb) potatoes, cooked and creamed
15 ml spoon (1 tbsp) cornflour

Beat the sliced beef with a rolling pin. Roll each slice round a frankfurter and tie with fine string or cotton.
Melt half the fat and brown the beef rolls on all sides. Remove the rolls from the pan and add remaining fat; sauté the vegetables until the fat is absorbed. Place the beef rolls on top, pour on the stock and season.
Bring to the boil, cover, then reduce heat and simmer for about 2 hours until the meat is tender.
Lift the beef rolls out and arrange in a ring of creamed potato. Keep hot. Strain the cooking liquid, thicken it with the cornflour and check the seasoning. Pour sauce over the beef rolls.

Beef and potato Charlotte

serves 4-5

1 kg (2 lb) potatoes, peeled and thinly sliced
25 g (1 oz) margarine
175 g (6 oz) onion, skinned and chopped
¼ kg (½ lb) minced beef
¼ kg (½ lb) belly of pork, minced
3 tomatoes, skinned and sliced
50 g (2 oz) fresh white breadcrumbs
2 × 15 ml spoons (2 level tbsps) tomato paste
large pinch mixed herbs
salt and freshly ground black pepper
1 egg, beaten
50 g (2 oz) cheese, grated

Cook the potatoes in boiling salted water for 2 minutes. Drain

and set aside to cool. Sauté the onion in the margarine, combine it with the rest of the ingredients, except the egg and cheese. Grease a 21.5 cm (8½ in) spring-release tin with a plain base and stand it on a baking tray. Arrange potatoes, overlapping, in the base and around the sides. Brush with egg. Pack in half the meat, top with more potato, the rest of the meat and finally potato. Press down well, sprinkle with cheese and bake at 220°C (425°F) mark 7, for about 1¼ hours. Remove the tin, brush potatoes with more beaten egg and cook for a further 15 minutes or until golden.

Lamb Julienne

serves 6

3 × 15 ml spoons (3 level tbsps) flour
5 ml spoon (1 level tsp) curry powder
10 ml spoon (2 level tsps) salt
freshly ground black pepper
1 kg (2 lb) boned shoulder lamb, cubed
oil for frying
900 ml (1½ pints) water or chicken stock
8 small onions, skinned
8 carrots, peeled

For crispy dumplings:
40 g (1½ oz) butter
50 g (2 oz) fresh white breadcrumbs
225 g (8 oz) self-raising flour
5 ml spoon (1 level tsp) salt
2.5 ml spoon (½ level tsp) dried onion
3 × 15 ml spoons (3 tbsps) corn oil
milk

Sift together the flour, curry powder, salt and pepper. Toss the lamb cubes in this mixture. Fry the meat in the oil until well browned.
Stir in any excess flour. Gradually add the water or stock, stirring, and bring to the boil. Transfer to a casserole and add the onions. Cover and cook in the oven at 170°C (325°F) mark 3 for 1 hour.
Cut the carrots into long, thick matchsticks and add to the meat.

Lamb Julienne

For crispy dumplings, melt the butter in a pan, stir in the crumbs and cook gently, stirring frequently, until golden. Sift together the flour, salt and onion powder. Add crumb mixture. Stir in the oil and enough milk to give a soft but manageable dough. Shape into balls, coat with crumbs and arrange in the casserole. Cover and cook for a further hour.

Boiled lamb with dill sauce

serves 3-4

1 kg (2 lb) best end neck of lamb
15 ml spoon (1 level tbsp) salt
3-4 peppercorns
1 bay leaf
a sprig of dill

For dill sauce:
50 g (2 oz) butter
50 g (2 oz) plain flour
600 ml (1 pint) stock
3 × 15 ml spoons (3 level tbsps) chopped fresh dill
2 × 15 ml spoons (2 tbsps) vinegar
10 ml spoon (2 level tsps) sugar
1 egg yolk
salt and pepper

Put the lamb in a pan and cover with about 1.1 litre (2 pints) water. Add the seasonings and herbs and simmer for 1–1½ hours, until the meat is tender. Melt the butter in a pan, stir in the flour and gradually add the stock. Simmer for 2–3 minutes, stirring all the time. Add 2 × 15 ml spoons (2 tbsps) of the dill, the vinegar and the sugar. Remove from the heat and stir in the egg yolk and seasoning.
Place the well drained lamb on a serving dish, pour the sauce over and sprinkle with remaining dill.

Navarin of lamb

serves 4

1 kg (2 lb) middle neck of lamb, trimmed

Boiled lamb, served Norwegian-style, with dill sauce

50 g (2 oz) lard or dripping
2 × 15 ml spoons (2 level tbsps) flour
10 ml spoon (2 level tsps) salt
2.5 ml spoon (½ level tsp) pepper
3 × 15 ml spoon (3 level tbsps) tomato paste
600 ml (1 pint) hot water
bouquet garni (including cut clove garlic)
4 onions, skinned and sliced
4 carrots, peeled and sliced
4 small turnips, peeled and sliced
8 small potatoes, peeled

Cut the meat into serving-size pieces. Melt 25 g (1 oz) fat in a pan and brown the meat a few pieces at a time. Dredge with seasoned flour and brown again. Gradually stir in the tomato paste and hot water, add the bouquet garni, bring to the boil, reduce heat, cover and simmer for 1 hour.
Melt 25 g (1 oz) fat in a pan and fry all the vegetables except the potatoes. When lightly browned add to the meat and simmer for a further 30 minutes. Discard the bouquet garni, add the potatoes and simmer for a further 30 minutes. Adjust seasoning and skim off fat. Spoon the meat and vegetables into serving dish.

Oxtail with mustard dumplings

serves 6

1 oxtail (1 kg (2 lb)) chopped in small pieces
2 × 15 ml spoons (2 tbsps) cooking oil
100 g (4 oz) celery, trimmed and diced
100 g (4 oz) carrots, peeled and diced
1 small turnip, peeled and diced
1.8 litres (3 pints) rich beef stock
5 ml (1 level tsp) salt
freshly ground black pepper
bouquet garni
2.5 ml spoon (½ tsp) gravy browning
5 ml spoon (1 level tsp) concentrated curry sauce
300–400 ml (½–¾ pint) beef stock

For the dumplings:
75 g (3 oz) self-raising flour
5 ml spoon (1 level tsp) dry mustard
40 g (1½ oz) shredded suet
2.5 ml (½ level tsp) salt

freshly ground black pepper
water

Wipe the oxtail with a damp cloth and remove any excess fat. Place the meat in a frying pan with the oil and fry briskly to seal. Drain and place in a large saucepan. Fry the vegetables in the reheated meat residue for 3–4 minutes or until lightly browned.

Add to the meat. Pour the stock over, season well, add the bouquet garni, then cover and simmer for about 4 hours. Strain and discard the bouquet garni. Chill the meat juices to allow the fat to set; remove the fat and take all the flesh from the bones. Reheat the meat juices and vegetables and purée them in an electric blender. Return to pan and stir in last three ingredients – gravy browning, concentrated curry sauce and stock. Bring to the boil, reduce the heat, check seasoning and add the dumplings. Cook for about 30 minutes more.

To make the dumplings: Sift the flour and mustard together, then stir in the suet, salt and pepper. Add water to mix to give a firm dough. Shape into about 20 small balls.

Rolled stuffed breast of lamb

serves 4

1½ kg (3 lb) breast of lamb, boned
salt and freshly ground black
* pepper*
100 g (4 oz) lean veal
75 g (3 oz) lean bacon
25 g (1 oz) butter
1 onion, skinned and finely
* chopped*
75 g (3 oz) fresh white
* breadcrumbs*
1 large mushroom, washed and
* chopped*
5 ml spoon (1 level tsp) finely
* chopped parsley*
cayenne pepper
ground mace
1 egg, beaten
milk, optional

Spread the boned joint out flat on a board, sprinkle with salt and pepper and rub the seasonings into the meat.

Pass the mixed veal and bacon twice through a mincer, then beat them well in a bowl. Lightly fry the onion in a little of the butter, until soft but not coloured. Add to the meat. Add the breadcrumbs, mushroom, remaining butter, and parsley; season with salt, pepper and a very little cayenne and mace. Lastly, bind with the beaten egg. Mix well, and if the mixture is too stiff add a little milk to give the mixture a looser consistency.

Spread the veal forcemeat over the lamb and roll the meat up loosely to allow the stuffing to expand during cooking. Tie the roll in several places with fine string, to hold its shape. Weigh it and calculate the cooking time, allowing 27–30 minutes per ½ kg (1 lb) plus 27 minutes. Place the meat in the roasting tin, putting it on a grill grid or meat trivet if it is fatty, and cook in the centre of the oven at 180°C (350°F) mark 4 for the calculated time.

Remove the string and serve sliced fairly thickly, accompanied by a thickened gravy. Any stuffing left over can be cooked in a separate small dish and served with the joint.

Summer lamb casserole

serves 4

1 kg (2 lb) neck of lamb
10 ml spoon (2 level tsps) salt
2.5 ml spoon (½ level tsp) pepper
½ kg (1 lb) carrots, scraped
* and sliced*
½ kg (1 lb) small new potatoes,
* scraped*
225 g (½ lb) frozen peas or fresh
* peas, shelled*
15 ml spoon (1 level tbsp) tomato
* paste*
fresh mint, chopped

Place the meat in a shallow flame-proof casserole, cover with cold water and bring to the boil. Pour off the water, rinse the meat and return it to the casserole with 600 ml (1 pint) cold water, to which the salt and pepper has been added. Bring to the boil, add the carrots, cover and cook in the oven at 170°C (325°F) mark 3 for about 1½ hours, until the meat is fork tender.

Add the potatoes to the casserole

Use the tender, sweet vegetables of summer for Summer lamb casserole

with the peas, if fresh are used; cover and cook for a further 20 minutes. Remove the meat and strip the flesh from the bones. Cut it roughly and return it to the casserole with the peas and tomato paste. Adjust seasoning and return the casserole to the oven for a further 10–15 minutes. To serve, sprinkle with chopped mint.

Lamb and potato pasties

serves 4

15 ml spoon (1 tbsp) oil
225 g (8 oz) potatoes, peeled and diced
1 small onion, skinned and diced
350 g (12 oz) boned, lean shoulder of lamb, coarsely minced
1 beef stock cube
salt and freshly ground black pepper
375 g (13 oz) pkt. frozen puff pastry, thawed
milk to glaze

Heat the oil in a frying-pan and gently fry the potato and onion for 3–4 minutes. Lift out using a draining spoon. Fry meat quickly to seal, then mix with potato, onion, crumbled stock cube, salt and pepper. Cool. Roll out pastry thinly and cut out four 18 cm (7 in) rounds, using a saucepan lid as a guide. Divide the filling between the rounds, brush the edges with milk, then bring the pastry up and seal on top by pressing together with fingertips.
Place the pasties on a baking sheet, brush with milk and bake at 220°C (425°F) mark 7 for 15 minutes then reduce the heat to 180°C (350°F) mark 4 for a further 20–25 minutes.

Equally as good hot or cold, serve Lamb and potato pasties hot for supper or cold for a picnic

Barbecued pork chops

serves 4

4 lean spare rib pork chops, trimmed of fat
salt and pepper
2 × 15 ml spoons (2 tbsps) clear honey
2 × 15 ml spoons (2 tbsps) soy sauce
15 ml spoon (1 level tbsp) tomato ketchup
1 small clove garlic, skinned and crushed
½ × 2.5 ml spoon (¼ level tsp) dry mustard
juice of 1 large orange
juice of ½ small lemon
4 × 15 ml spoons (4 tbsps) vinegar
15 ml spoon (1 tbsp) cooking oil
1 small onion, skinned and chopped

Season the chops well. In a bowl, mix together the honey, soy sauce, tomato ketchup, garlic, mustard, fruit juices and vinegar. In a saucepan, heat the oil and fry the chops quickly on both sides until brown. Drain off all fat and add the sauce mixture and onion. Cover and simmer for 45 minutes, or until the chops are really tender. Serve at once.

Moussaka

serves 6

1 kg (2 lb) aubergines, trimmed and thinly sliced
salt
8–10 × 15 ml spoons (8–10 tbsps) olive or vegetable oil
50 g (2 oz) butter
3 medium-sized onions, skinned and thinly sliced
1 kg (2 lb) lean lamb, minced
50 g (2 oz) tomato paste
seasoning
425 g (15 oz) can of plum tomatoes
a bay leaf
600 ml (1 pint) cheese sauce
a little Parmesan cheese, grated
chopped parsley for garnish

Spread out the aubergines in a large plate or tray, sprinkle with salt and leave for at least an hour. Rinse them under cold, running water and dry the slices with absorbent kitchen paper. Fry the aubergines in batches in the oil for about 10 minutes, turning them frequently. Meanwhile, melt the butter in another pan and sauté the onion until soft.
Place the minced lamb in a bowl and stir in the tomato paste and seasoning. Pass the plum tomatoes with their juice through a sieve, or purée them in an electric blender. In a large ovenproof casserole, arrange layers of aubergine, lamb and onion, adding the bay leaf and finishing with aubergine. Pour the tomato purée over (there should be enough room left for the cheese sauce). Cover and cook in the oven at 180°C (350°F) mark 4 for 1 hour.
Pour the cheese sauce over the moussaka and sprinkle with the Parmesan cheese. Replace dish in the oven and cook uncovered for about a further ½ hour, until the sauce is golden. Garnish with parsley. Remove bay leaf.

Braised pork and red cabbage

serves 6

1 kg (2 lb) unsalted belly pork, rinded
15 g (½ oz) butter
15 ml spoon (1 tbsp) cooking oil
salt and freshly ground black pepper
½ kg (1 lb) cooking apples, peeled and cored
½ kg (1 lb) red cabbage, trimmed and finely shredded
2 × 15 ml spoons (2 level tbsps) flour
3 × 15 ml spoons (3 tbsps) wine vinegar
600 ml (1 pint) stock

Cut the pork away from the bone in one piece, then cut it into strips 1 cm (½ in) wide. Cut each strip in half. In a frying pan, melt the butter with the oil and heat until bubbling. Season the pork and fry until well browned on both sides. Reduce heat and cook for a further 10–15 minutes. Slice the apples roughly. Place a good third of the red cabbage in a deep casserole, add some apple and half of meat. Continue to make layers, finishing with the apple. Blend the flour with the vinegar, gradually add the stock until blended and adjust the seasoning. Bring to the boil, stirring, and cook for 2–3 minutes before pouring into the casserole. Cook, covered, at 180°C (350°F) mark 4 for about 2 hours, or until the pork is tender.

Pigaleekie

serves 4

15 g (½ oz) butter
½ kg (1 lb) lean pork, minced
1 clove garlic, skinned and crushed
¼ kg (½ lb) leeks, washed and cut into large pieces
1 small red pepper, seeded and finely diced
400 ml (¾ pint) stock
salt and pepper
5 × 15 ml spoons (5 level tbsps) long grain rice
gravy browning
parsley, chopped

Heat the butter in a shallow flameproof casserole, stir in the pork and cook quickly for 5 minutes. Drain off the fat. Add the garlic, leeks, red pepper and stock. Season well, cover and cook in the oven at 170°C (325°F) mark 3 for 1 hour.
Stir in the rice and simmer on top of the stove for a further 15–20 minutes. Sprinkle with chopped parsley just before serving.

Pork chop braise

serves 4

4 pork chops (about 2 cm (¾ in) thick)
15 ml spoon (1 level tbsp) flour
15 ml spoon (1 tbsp) cooking oil
2 × 15 ml spoons (2 tbsps) honey
150 ml (¼ pint) water, boiling
large pinch ground cloves
2 oranges
1 onion, skinned and chopped
25 g (1 oz) butter
100 g (4 oz) mushrooms, sliced

Remove any excess fat from the chops and coat them in flour.

Pork chop braise is a winner. Serve with Variety rice (page 69).

Heat the oil in a large saucepan and fry the chops 2 at a time on both sides until golden brown. As each is browned, remove from the pan, drain on absorbent kitchen paper and keep warm.
Meanwhile, dissolve the honey in the water, stir in the cloves and the juice of 1 orange.
When the chops are all browned, fry the onion in the oil until soft, drain off as much fat as possible and stir in any remaining flour. Add the honey mixture and stir well. Replace the chops, bring to the boil, cover and simmer for 45 minutes, or until the chops are really tender.
Meanwhile sauté the mushrooms in the butter. Peel the remaining orange and divide into segments, free of membrane. Stir the mushrooms and orange into the chops 10 minutes before serving. Arrange chops on a serving dish and pour over the sauce.

Pork ragoût

serves 4

50 g (2 oz) fat or oil
2 onions, skinned and sliced

1 kg (2 lb) shoulder of pork, boned and cubed
2 small green peppers, deseeded and sliced
2 cloves of garlic, crushed
150 ml (¼ pint) white wine
300 ml (½ pint) stock
½ × 2.5 ml spoon (¼ level tsp) chilli powder
5 ml spoon (1 level tsp) celery salt
1 bay leaf
salt and pepper
40 g (1½ oz) long grain rice
75 g (3 oz) pkt. sage and onion stuffing mix

Cook the onions gently in the fat for about 5 minutes; remove from the pan and brown the meat in the remaining fat for 8–10 minutes; drain off any excess fat. Return the onions to the pan with the peppers, garlic, wine, stock, chilli powder (a little at a time according to taste), celery salt, bay leaf and seasoning. Cover and simmer for 1½ hours, or until the meat is tender. Meanwhile cook the rice in boiling salted water for 15–20 minutes and drain well. Make up the sage and onion stuffing according to the directions on the packet, shape into 12 small balls and fry until pale golden brown – 3–4 minutes. Add to the meat with the rice just before serving.

Pork chops with creamed cabbage

serves 6

1½ kg (3 lb) cabbage, trimmed and shredded
400 ml (¾ pint) low fat natural yoghurt
salt and freshly ground black pepper
6 pork chops
cooking oil
sage
3 × 15 ml spoons (3 tbsps) stock
40 g (1½ oz) cheese, grated
paprika

Plunge the shredded cabbage into boiling salted water; bring to the boil again and blanch for 3 minutes. Drain. Add the yoghurt and some pepper; toss the mixture together lightly.
Place half the cabbage in a shallow casserole, large enough to take the chops in a single layer.

Brush the chops with oil and grill until golden, turning. Arrange in a single layer on the cabbage and season lightly.

Add a sprinkling of sage and the stock to the grill-pan drippings, stirring well to loosen any residue. Spoon the liquid evenly over the chops and cover with the remaining cabbage.

Cook in the oven at 180°C (350°F) mark 4 for about ¾ hour. If there is too much liquid, drain it off and reduce it to the required amount by fast boiling in a separate pan; return it to the casserole. Just before serving, sprinkle the top with the cheese.

Garnish with a dusting of paprika. Serve with small jacket potatoes and carrot slices.

Pork chops with creamed cabbage – simple to make and delicious

Orange-braised pork chops

serves 4

75 g (3 oz) butter
¼ kg (½ lb) onions, skinned and sliced
4 pork chops
salt and pepper
5 ml spoon (1 level tsp) dry mustard
10 ml spoon (2 level tsps) demerara sugar
15 ml spoon (1 level tbsp) plain flour
3 large oranges
150 ml (¼ pint) stock

In a frying pan, heat 25 g (1 oz) butter, add the onions and fry gently until light golden brown. Remove them from the pan. Trim any excess fat from the chops.

In a small bowl, mix together the salt and pepper, mustard, sugar and remaining 50 g (2 oz) butter. Spread on one side of each chop. Fry the chops until golden on both sides. Remove from pan, add flour to the juices and mix well. Coarsely grate the rind from 2 oranges and add to the pan with the onions. Squeeze the juice from 2 oranges and make up to 150 ml (¼ pint) with water. Add to the pan, stirring, then add the stock and bring to the boil.

Peel remaining orange and cut it into segments. Arrange the chops in a flameproof pan, add the orange segments. Pour on the sauce. Cover and simmer on top of the stove for 40 minutes.

Pork risotto

serves 4

25 g (1 oz) butter
175 g (6 oz) Italian rice
1 small onion, skinned and chopped
10 ml spoon (2 level tsps) curry powder
400–600 ml (¾–1 pint) chicken or turkey stock
salt and pepper
100 g (4 oz) frozen peas
½ kg (1 lb) large pork sausages
1 cooking apple, peeled, cored and diced
2 tomatoes, peeled and deseeded

Melt the butter and fry the rice, onion and curry powder for 5 minutes, stirring frequently. Add the stock, bring to the boil, adjust seasoning, cover and simmer for 10 minutes. Add the peas and continue cooking until all the stock has been absorbed. If you prefer, the peas can be cooked separately.

Meanwhile, cook the sausages until golden by grilling, frying or baking. Slice into thick rings with a sharp knife and keep hot. Add the apple and diced tomato to the rice, folding them in with a fork. Arrange the sausage (and the peas, if cooked separately) in layers with the rice mixture in a hot dish.

Veal fricassée

serves 4

½–¾ kg (1–1½ lb) stewing veal

225 g (½ lb) bacon rashers, in one piece
25 g (1 oz) butter
15 ml spoon (1 tbsp) oil
½ small onion, skinned and finely chopped
300 ml (½ pint) veal stock or water
salt and pepper
kneaded butter (40 g (1½ oz) flour worked into 40 g (1½ oz) softened butter)
2 × 15 ml spoons (2 tbsps) lemon juice
2 slices white bread
parsley for garnish

Cut the veal into even 2.5 cm (1 in) cubes. Rind and trim the bacon and cut as for the veal. Heat the butter with the oil and fry the veal and bacon until pale brown. Remove the meat and place in a large casserole. Add the onion to the fat, fry and add to the casserole. Pour over the stock or water, season and cover. Cook in the oven at 180°C (350°F) mark 4 for 1½ hours. Strain off the liquor into a small pan, keeping the meat hot in the casserole. Drop small pieces of the kneaded butter into the hot liquor, stir well to thicken, bring to the boil and boil for 2–3 minutes. Add the lemon juice and adjust seasoning. Pour the sauce over the veal.

Toast the bread slices, cut into triangular croûtes and use to garnish the veal, with the parsley.

Veal fricassée with Baked tomatoes (page 67) and potatoes

Veal and rice paprika

serves 4

25 g (1 oz) butter
½ kg (1 lb) pie veal, cut into small pieces
175 g (6 oz) onions, skinned and finely sliced
5 ml spoon (1 level tsp) paprika
15 ml spoon (1 level tbsp) tomato paste
400 ml (¾ pint) stock
175 g (6 oz) long grain rice
150 ml (¼ pint) sour cream
salt and pepper
chopped parsley for garnish

Melt the butter in a frying pan. When on the point of turning brown, add the veal and fry briskly. Transfer the meat to a casserole and fry the onion until tender. Stir in the paprika, tomato paste and stock. Pour over the veal, cover and cook in the oven at 170°C (325°F) mark 3 for about 1 hour, or until tender. Add the rice, cover and return to the oven for a further 30 minutes.

Gently heat the sour cream in a small pan and fork it through the rice. Season and sprinkle with chopped parsley.

Rich casseroled heart

serves 4

1 ox heart (1¼–1½ kg (2½–3 lb))
50 g (2 oz) fat or oil
2 onions, skinned and sliced
25 g (1 oz) flour
300 ml (½ pint) stock
¼ kg (½ lb) carrots, peeled and grated
½ small swede, peeled and grated
pared rind of 1 orange
6 walnuts, chopped

Slice the heart, removing the tubes, and wash it well. Fry in fat or oil until slightly brown, then put into a casserole. Fry the onions and add to the casserole. Add the flour to the remaining fat and brown slightly. Pour in the stock, bring to the boil, stirring, and simmer for 2–3 minutes, then

Veal and rice paprika, finished with sour cream

strain over the meat in the casserole. Cover and cook at 150°C (300°F) mark 2 for 2½–3 hours. Add the carrots and swede and cook for a further hour. Shred the orange rind and boil for 10–15 minutes; drain. Add the walnuts and orange rind to the casserole for the last 15 minutes.

Cheese topped gammon

serves 4

4 gammon rashers (about 175 g (6 oz) each)

Cheese topped gammon: lemon juice prevents apples browning

a little melted butter
2 green eating apples
lemon juice
175 g (6 oz) Cheddar cheese, thinly sliced

Rind the gammon and snip the fat in four or five places on each rasher. Line the grill pan with foil and lay the rashers side by side on the foil. Grill for 4–5 minutes, turning halfway through cooking time. Wipe and core the apples, but do not peel; slice thinly across in rounds. Lay the apple slices over the gammon. Sprinkle the apples with a little lemon juice. Brush a little melted butter over the apple slices and continue grilling for 2–3 minutes. Lay the cheese slices over the apple and return to the grill for a further 1 minute.

Braised sweetbreads

serves 4

½ kg (1 lb) lambs' sweetbreads
15 ml spoon (1 tbsp) cooking oil
1 large carrot, peeled and diced
1 onion, skinned and diced
2 celery stalks, scrubbed and diced
salt and freshly ground black pepper
300 ml (½ pint) white stock
75 g (3 oz) green streaky bacon rashers, rinded
10 ml spoon (2 level tsps) cornflour
parsley for garnish

Soak the sweetbreads for at least 4 hours, changing the water several times. Put into fresh cold water and bring to the boil; lift the sweetbreads out and rinse under running cold water. Remove the black veins and skin, wrap lightly in a cloth or muslin and cool, pressed between 2 weighted plates. Fry the prepared vegetables in the oil until half cooked. Place them in the base of a casserole which is just large enough to take the sweetbreads. Add the seasoning and stock (just enough to cover the vegetables) and arrange the sliced sweetbreads on top. Overlap the rashers of bacon on top.

Cover and cook in the oven at 190°C (375°F) mark 5 for ½–¾ hour, basting occasionally with the juices. Increase the oven temperature to 220°C (425°F) mark 7 and remove the lid for the last 10 minutes.

Strain the liquor from the casserole. Thicken it with the cornflour and pour over the sweetbreads. Garnish with parsley.

Ragoût of liver

serves 4

½ kg (1 lb) lambs' liver
4 × 15 ml spoons (4 level tbsps) seasoned flour
25 g (1 oz) fat or oil
1 onion, skinned and sliced
4 rashers bacon, chopped
400 ml (¾ pint) stock
25 g (1 oz) sultanas

1 apple, peeled and grated
5 ml spoon (1 level tsp) tomato
  paste
225 g (8 oz) long grain rice

Wash and trim the liver, cut it
into small pieces and coat with
the seasoned flour. Fry the liver,
onion and bacon in the fat or oil
until golden brown. Add the
stock to the pan and bring to the
boil, stirring constantly. Add the
sultanas, apple and tomato paste
and simmer for 20 minutes.
Cook the rice in boiling salted
water until tender and serve separately.

Garnish Spiced orange gammon with the orange slices before glazing

Spiced orange gammon

serves 6

1½ kg (3 lb) middle gammon joint
75 g (3 oz) butter
65 g (2½ oz) soft brown sugar
grated rind and juice of
  1½ oranges

3 × 15 ml spoons (3 tbsps) cider
  vinegar
½ × 2.5 ml spoon (¼ level tsp)
  ground ginger
salt
freshly ground black pepper
1 whole orange

Soak gammon in cold water for
2–3 hours. Drain and place skin
side down in a large pan; cover
with fresh water. Bring to the
boil, skim off the scum, reduce

the heat and cook for 35 minutes.
Make sure that the joint is always
covered with water, topping it up
with fresh boiling water if necessary. Drain the joint. Wrap it in
foil and place in a roasting tin.
Continue to cook in the oven at
180°C (350°F) mark 4 for about
35 minutes.
Meanwhile, prepare the orange
glaze. Melt the butter and sugar
over a low heat. When the sugar is
dissolved, raise the heat and cook

until golden. Remove from the
heat and add the rind and juice of
the oranges, vinegar and ginger.
Continue to heat gently, uncovered, for 7–10 minutes. Adjust
seasoning.
Slice the whole orange and poach
in water to cover until the rind is
soft. Drain and add to the orange
caramel. Continue to heat gently
for a further 5 minutes to infuse
the flavours.
About 20 minutes before the end
of the cooking time, remove the
gammon from the oven, unwrap
the foil and strip off the rind. Coat
the fat with some orange glaze
and slices. Return it to the oven
and raise the temperature to
220°C (425°F) mark 7. Cook for a
further 20 minutes.
Serve the gammon hot, with the
rest of the glaze separately.

Savoury liver

serves 4

½ kg (1 lb) lambs' liver
50 g (2 oz) fresh white
  breadcrumbs

Serve Ragoût of liver on a bed of rice or serve rice separately

*15 ml spoon (1 level tbsp) chopped
  parsley*
*5 ml spoon (1 level tsp) mixed
  dried herbs*
25 g (1 oz) suet, chopped
salt and pepper
grated rind of ½ lemon
little egg or milk to mix
4 rashers streaky bacon, rinded
150 ml (¼ pint) stock or water

Wash and slice the liver and
arrange it in a casserole. Mix
together the breadcrumbs, parsley, herbs, suet, seasoning and
lemon rind. Bind with a little egg
or milk. Spread the stuffing on
the liver and place the bacon on
top. Pour in the stock or water and
cover. Cook in the oven at 180°C
(350°F) mark 4 for 30–45
minutes, until the liver is tender,
removing the lid for the final 15
minutes to crisp the bacon.

Liver and bacon provençale

serves 4

½ kg (1 lb) lambs' liver
50 g (2 oz) flour
*2 × 15 ml spoons (2 tbsps) cooking
  oil*
*¼ kg (½ lb) lean streaky bacon
  rashers, rinded and chopped*
*½ kg (1 lb) onions, skinned and
  chopped*
400 g (14 oz) can plum tomatoes
*5 ml spoon (1 level tsp) dried
  marjoram*
1 bay leaf
*15 ml spoon (1 tbsp)
  Worcestershire sauce*

*400 ml (¾ pint) brown stock
  or 400 ml (¾ pint) water
  and beef stock cube*
*salt and freshly ground black
  pepper*

Slice the liver into fairly large
strips, coat with flour and fry in
oil until golden brown. Place in a
casserole.
Add the bacon and onions to the
frying pan and cook until golden.
Stir in any flour left over from
coating the liver. Add the
tomatoes, marjoram, bay leaf and
Worcestershire sauce. Stir in the
stock, season well, place in the
casserole. Cover with a tightly
fitting lid and cook in the oven at
150°C (300°F) mark 2 for about
1½ hours. Serve with a green
salad and noodles (cooked in boiling salted water, drained and tossed in butter and pepper).

Meatballs and rice hotpot

serves 4

*6 × 15 ml spoons (6 tbsps) long
  grain rice*
*400 g (14 oz) can whole carrots,
  drained*
400 g (14 oz) can plum tomatoes
*15 ml spoon (1 tbsp) dried onion
  flakes*
5 ml spoon (1 level tsp) salt
*5 ml spoon (1 level tsp) mixed
  herbs*
pepper
½ kg (1 lb) beef, minced
300 ml (½ pint) water

Don't forget to remove the bay leaf from Liver and bacon provençale before serving

Stuffed heart casserole served with potatoes and cabbage

Put the rice, carrots, tomatoes, and seasonings into a 1.8–2.3 litre (3–4 pint) casserole and stir well. Shape the minced beef into small balls and place on top of the rice mixture. Sprinkle with salt and pepper, pour in the liquid and cover. Cook in the centre of the oven at 180°C (350°F) mark 4 for 2 hours.

Pot roast veal

serves 6

1½ kg (3 lb) shoulder of veal,
  boned and rolled
salt and pepper
50 g (2 oz) butter
15 ml spoon (1 tbsp) cooking oil
1 small onion, skinned and sliced
6 small carrots, peeled and sliced
300 ml (½ pint) water
a little dried thyme
cornflour

Wipe the meat and season well. Melt the butter with the oil in a frying pan. Lightly brown the meat all over. Transfer the meat to a casserole and keep hot.
Fry the vegetables until brown, add the water, bring to the boil and then pour round the meat in the casserole. Add the thyme. Cover and cook at 180°C (350°F) mark 4 for about 2½ hours, until the meat is tender.
Slice the meat and arrange on a serving dish. Thicken the sauce with a little cornflour and pour over the meat.

Stuffed heart casserole

serves 4

4 small lambs' hearts
2 × 15 ml spoons (2 level tbsps)
  seasoned flour
25 g (1 oz) fat or oil
600 ml (1 pint) stock
1 onion, skinned and sliced
4 celery stalks, scrubbed and sliced
100 g (¼ lb) carrots, peeled and
  sliced
15 ml spoon (1 tbsp) cider
  (optional)

For stuffing:
100 g (4 oz) breadcrumbs
1 medium-sized onion, skinned
  and finely chopped
3 × 15 ml spoons (3 tbsps) melted
  butter
10 ml spoon (2 level tsps) mixed
  dried herbs
salt and pepper

Wash the hearts, slit open, remove any tubes and wash again. Mix the ingredients for stuffing and fill the hearts with it. Tie them into their original shape with string, coat with seasoned flour and brown quickly in the hot fat or oil.
Place in a casserole with the stock, cover and cook in the oven at 180°C (350°F) mark 4 for 2½ hours, turning them frequently. Add the onion, celery, carrots and cider (if used) for the last 45 minutes.

Faggots – an old-fashioned favourite

Faggots

serves 4·6

½ kg (1 lb) pig's liver
175 g (6 oz) onion, skinned
275 g (10 oz) fresh white
  breadcrumbs
75 g (3 oz) shredded suet
salt
freshly ground black pepper
2.5 ml spoon (½ level tsp) chopped
  sage
15 ml spoon (1 level tbsp) flour
600 ml (1 pint) rich beef stock
chopped parsley

Mince the liver and onion together, add the breadcrumbs and suet and combine fully together. Season well with salt, pepper and sage. Shape into balls on a well floured surface. Place each faggot in a small square of buttered foil. Enclose them loosely and place on a baking sheet. Bake in centre of oven at 180°C (350°F) mark 4 for about 30 minutes. Remove the faggots from the foil; place them in a flameproof casserole.

To make the gravy, place the flour in a small bowl and blend to a cream with a little of the stock. Add remaining stock and pour round the faggots. Heat gently, turning the faggots, until the gravy thickens. Cook for 5–10 minutes, then garnish with parsley and serve.

Note: *Foil replaces the caul which was originally used but is now difficult to obtain.*

Devilled gammon with pineapple

serves 4

2 gammon rashers (about 350 g
  (12 oz) each)
4 × 15 ml spoons (4 level tbsps)
  dry mustard
175 g (6 oz) light, soft brown sugar
225 g (8 oz) can pineapple rings
8 maraschino cherries

Trim the rind from the gammon rashers and snip the fat at intervals. Mix together the mustard, sugar and 8 × 15 ml spoons (8 tbsps) syrup from the can of pineapple. Lay the gammon on the grill rack, spread evenly with some of the sugar mixture and cook under a medium grill for 15 minutes, basting every 5 minutes with the pan drippings.

Turn the gammon, spread with remaining sugar mixture and cook for a further 15 minutes. Place 2 pineapple rings and 4 cherries on each rasher; baste, and cook for a further 5 minutes. If the fat shows signs of over-browning, cover the area with a piece of kitchen foil. Each rasher will serve 2 people. Serve with spinach and potatoes.

Note: *If the gammon tends to be salty, leave it to soak in cold water for an hour before cooking, then pat it dry.*

Fried sweetbreads

serves 4

½ kg (1 lb) lambs' or calves'
 sweetbreads
juice of ½ lemon
beaten egg
breadcrumbs for coating
oil for deep-frying
tomato slices and onion rings

Fried sweetbreads are delicious sprinkled with lemon juice

Soak the sweetbreads for 3–4 hours in cold water, then drain and put in a pan. Cover with cold water and lemon juice and bring slowly to the boil. Simmer for 5 minutes. Drain and leave in cold water until they are firm and cold. Prepare and clean the sweetbreads as for Braised Sweetbreads. Press the sweetbreads well between absorbent paper, slice and dip in the beaten egg and crumbs. Fry the sweetbreads in the hot fat until golden. Serve at once with tartare or tomato sauce and garnished with tomato slices and onion rings.

Sweetbread hotpot

serves 4

½ kg (1 lb) sweetbreads
25 g (1 oz) butter
1 onion, skinned and chopped
225 g (8 oz) peas, shelled
100 g (4 oz) mushrooms, wiped
 and sliced
50 g (2 oz) plain flour
600 ml (1 pint) white stock
salt and freshly ground black
 pepper
5 ml (1 level tsp) mixed herbs
toast to garnish

Soak the sweetbreads for 3–4 hours in cold water, then drain and put in a pan. Cover with cold water, bring slowly to the boil, then pour off the liquid. Clean. In a flameproof casserole, fry the onion, peas and mushrooms slowly for 5 minutes in the butter. Add the flour and stir until cooked. Add the stock slowly, season, sprinkle in the herbs and bring to the boil.

Chop the sweetbreads and add to the casserole. Cook at 170°C (325°F) mark 3 for about 2 hours. Serve garnished with triangles of toast.

Creamed sweetbreads

serves 4

½ kg (1 lb) sweetbreads, prepared
½ onion, skinned and chopped
1 carrot, peeled and chopped
few parsley stalks
½ bay leaf
salt and freshly ground black
 pepper
40 g (1½ oz) butter
40 g (1½ oz) flour
300 ml (½ pint) milk
squeeze of lemon juice
chopped parsley for garnish

Put the sweetbreads, vegetables, herbs and seasonings in a pan with water to cover and simmer gently until tender – about ¾–1 hour. Drain and keep hot, retaining 300 ml (½ pint) of the cooking liquid.
Melt the butter, stir in the flour and cook for 2–3 minutes. Remove the pan from the heat and gradually stir in the sweetbread liquid and milk. Bring to the boil and continue to stir until it thickens. Season well and add the lemon juice.
Reheat the sweetbreads in the sauce and serve sprinkled with parsley.

Bacon chops with brown lentils

serves 4

175 g (6 oz) large brown lentils
2 × 15 ml spoons (2 tbsps) corn oil
4 lean bacon chops, about 1 cm
 (½ in) thick

600 ml (1 pint) chicken stock
100 g (4 oz) onion, skinned and
 finely chopped
3 celery stalks, washed and sliced
100 g (4 oz) button mushrooms,
 wiped and sliced
salt and freshly ground black
 pepper

Soak the lentils overnight in cold water. Drain. Heat 15 ml (1 tbsp) oil and fry the bacon chops until golden on both sides. Drain off all fat and add enough stock to just cover the chops. Cover and simmer for 15 minutes. In another pan, heat remaining oil and sauté onion, celery and mushrooms for about 2 minutes. Drain the stock from the chops and pour it over the vegetables. Add the lentils and seasoning to taste. Cover and simmer for 15 minutes until lentils are tender. Meanwhile keep chops hot. Serve the chops on a bed of lentils.

Tomato-sausage bake

serves 4

½ kg (1 lb) pork sausages
1 egg, beaten
4 × 15 ml spoons (4 tbsps) thyme
 and parsley stuffing mix
25 g (1 oz) butter
225 g (8 oz) onion, skinned and
 sliced
3 celery stalks, scrubbed and sliced
corn oil
200 g (7 oz) can tomatoes
¾ kg (1½ lb) potatoes, peeled and
 sliced

Prick the skins of the sausages and roll them in the beaten egg, then in the dry stuffing mix. In a flameproof casserole, fry the onion rings and celery in the butter until soft but not coloured. Drain and keep to one side. Add enough corn oil to the casserole to cover the base and lightly brown the sausages. Drain off any excess fat.
Return the vegetables to the casserole and stir in the contents of the can of tomatoes. Lay the potatoes on top, bring to the boil, cover and cook in the oven at 190°C (375°F) mark 5 for about 40 minutes.

Tomato-sausage bake will become a firm, family favourite

Lancashire tripe and onions

serves 4

½ kg (1 lb) dressed tripe
225 g (½ lb) shallots or small
  onions
600 ml (1 pint) milk
25 g (1 oz) butter or margarine
15 ml (½ oz) flour
pinch salt
freshly ground black pepper
pinch ground nutmeg

Wash the tripe and cut it into strips. Boil some water, pour it over the onions, allow to stand for a few minutes and drain before peeling the onions. Put the tripe, onions and milk in a saucepan; simmer gently, uncovered, for 1–1½ hours or until tender. Melt the butter, stir in the flour and cook the roux for 1–2 minutes. Remove from the heat. Strain the milk from the tripe after cooking, gradually add it to the roux, blending them together until smooth. Season well with salt, pepper and nutmeg. Let the sauce simmer for about 5 minutes, stirring. Add the tripe and onions to the sauce and re-heat before placing in a serving dish. Serve with creamed potatoes.

Meat loaf

serves 4·6

¼ kg (8 oz) stewing veal
¼ kg (8 oz) lean stewing beef
¼ kg (8 oz) lean bacon, rinded

Meat loaf and salad

100 g (4 oz) onion, skinned
50 g (2 oz) carrot, peeled and
  grated
100 g (4 oz) tomatoes, skinned and
  chopped
8 × 15 ml spoons (8 level tbsps)
  thyme and parsley stuffing mix
5 ml spoon (1 level tsp) salt
freshly ground black pepper
1 egg, beaten

Put the veal, beef, bacon and onion through a mincer twice. Combine this mixture with the remaining ingredients.
Place the mixture on a piece of kitchen foil and shape it into a loaf about 7.5 × 18 cm (3 × 7 in). Wrap it neatly, place it in a baking dish or loaf tin and cook in the oven at 180°C (350°F) mark 4 for 1¼ hours; open the foil and cook for a further 1¼ hours.
Allow to cool then chill in the refrigerator. Garnish with a few cucumber twists.

Winter sausage casserole

serves 4

25 g (1 oz) lard
½ kg (1 lb) meaty pork sausages
½ kg (1 lb) carrots, thinly sliced
4 celery stalks, sliced
400 g (14 oz) can whole tomatoes
300 ml (½ pint) water
2 × 15 ml spoons (2 level tbsps)
  tomato paste
15 ml spoon (1 tbsp)
  Worcestershire sauce
salt and freshly ground black
  pepper
½ kg (1 lb) potatoes, peeled and
  diced

parsley or celery leaves to garnish

Melt the lard in a saucepan and brown the sausages. Add the carrots and celery and fry gently, stirring, for about 5 minutes. Add the tomatoes, water, tomato paste, Worcestershire sauce, salt and pepper and bring to the boil. Reduce the heat and simmer for ½ hour. Add the potatoes and continue to simmer until the potato is tender, but not disintegrating. Most of the liquid will have been absorbed during the cooking. Garnish with chopped parsley or celery leaves.

Pressed tongue

1 salted ox tongue weighing about
  2 kg (4 lb)
8 peppercorns
1 carrot, peeled and sliced
1 onion, skinned and studded with
  3 cloves
1 bay leaf

Wash the tongue, and allow it to soak for 24 hours if highly salted. Put the tongue into a saucepan, just cover with cold water, cover and bring to the boil. Remove any scum with a spoon. Add remaining ingredients. Bring to the boil again, reduce heat and simmer the tongue until thoroughly tender. Allow about 1 hour per ½ kg (1 lb). When cooked, plunge the tongue briefly into cold water. Ease off the skin while tongue is still hot and remove the small bones from the back of the tongue. Return meat to the cooking liquid to cool. When cold, curl the tongue into a round soufflé dish or deep cake tin lined with foil. The container used should be large enough to take the tongue, leaving a few gaps. Check that the cooking liquid will set when cold. If it does not set to a firm jelly, either reduce by boiling fast or add a little gelatine. Just cover the meat with cool, strained cooking liquid. Press either with a heavily weighted plate, or a tongue press. Chill until the juices have jellied and turn out.

Right: *home-pressed tongue makes your salads and sandwiches a treat*

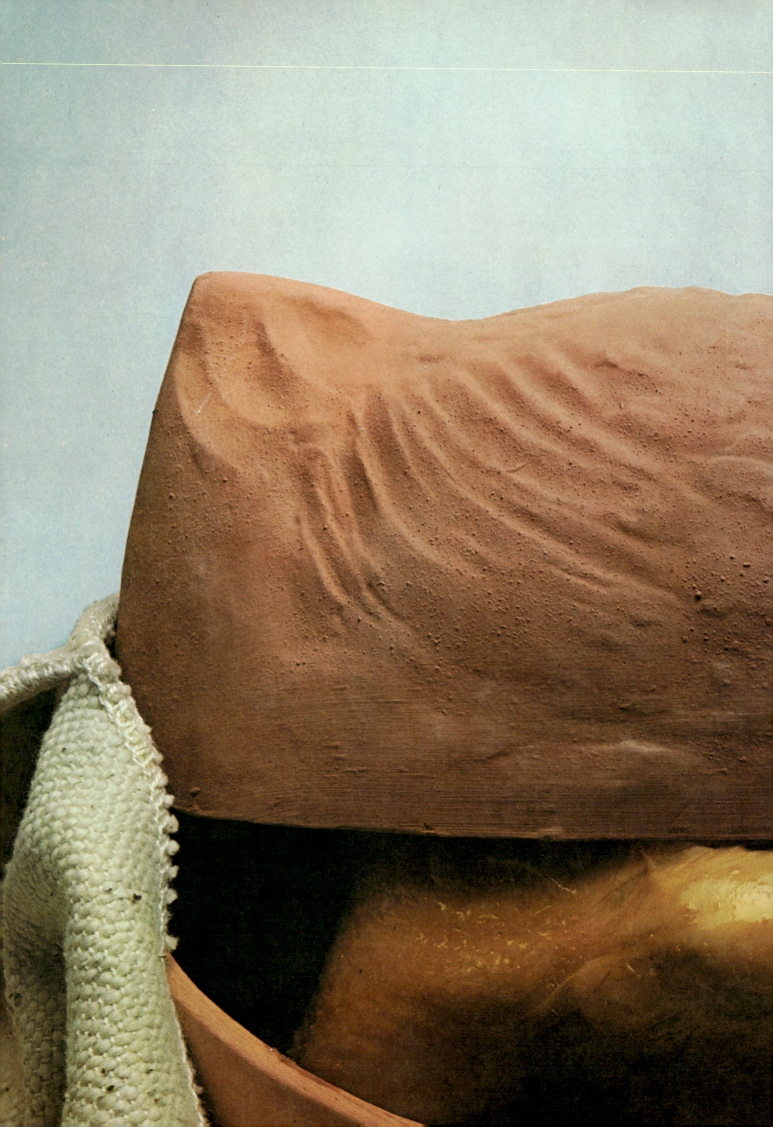

Chicken & Rabbit

simple and exotic ways
with chicken and rabbit

Chicken in a pot

serves 6

100 g (4 oz) pork sausage meat
2 × 15 ml spoons (2 tbsps) fresh
  white breadcrumbs
1 chicken liver, chopped
2 × 15 ml spoons (2 tbsps) chopped
  parsley
1¾ kg (3½ lb) oven-ready chicken
3 × 15 ml spoons (3 tbsps) cooking
  oil
salt and freshly ground black
  pepper
4 celery stalks, scrubbed and
  thickly sliced
2 leeks, washed and thinly sliced
225 g (½ lb) small turnips or
  swedes, peeled and quartered
225 g (½ lb) carrots, peeled and
  roughly sliced
juice of ½ lemon
a little stock made from the giblets
bouquet garni
chopped parsley to garnish

In a bowl, combine the sausage meat, breadcrumbs, liver and measured parsley. Stuff the chicken with this mixture and truss with skewers or string. Heat the oil in a large pan, season the skin of the bird with salt and pepper and fry lightly in the oil until golden brown on all sides.

Transfer the chicken to a large casserole. Put the celery, leek, turnip and carrot in the oil, cover and cook gently for 5 minutes, stirring often. Drain and pack round the chicken. Add the lemon juice and just enough stock to give a depth of about 2.5 cm (1 in) in the base of the casserole. Add the bouquet garni. Cover tightly, place on a baking sheet and cook in the oven at 180°C (350°F) mark 4 for about 1½ hours, until both the chicken and vegetables are fork tender. Arrange the chicken and drained vegetables on a large plate. Keep them warm in the oven. Skim off any surplus fat from the juices using a spoon and crumpled kitchen paper and reduce slightly. Adjust the seasoning and sprinkle in the parsley.

Pour the juice over the chicken and serve at once.

Full of flavour, Chicken in a pot makes a good family meal

Baked chicken with mushrooms

serves 4

4 chicken joints
salt and pepper
4 rashers streaky bacon, rinded
sprigs of parsley, washed
lemon rind
¼ kg (½ lb) button mushrooms,
  wiped

Place the chicken joints on separate squares of buttered kitchen foil and sprinkle with salt and pepper. Top each with a bacon rasher, a sprig of parsley and a small piece of lemon rind. Divide the mushrooms between the parcels and wrap securely, making the joins in the foil at the top. Place on a baking sheet and cook just above the centre of the oven at 200°C (400°F) mark 6 for 40 minutes. Open up the parcels a little and cook for a further 15–20 minutes to allow the bacon and top of the chicken to brown.

Roast chicken

Wipe the inside of the bird with a clean, damp cloth and stuff the neck end. Don't stuff too tightly as the forcemeat mixture tends to swell and might split the skin.
To add flavour if left unstuffed, put a knob of butter with some herbs, an onion or a wedge of lemon in the body. Truss. Brush the chicken with oil or melted butter and sprinkle with salt and pepper. Place a few strips of streaky bacon over the breast if you wish.
Cook at 190°C (375°F) mark 5, allowing 20 minutes per ½ kg (1 lb) plus 20 minutes. Baste occasionally and put a piece of greaseproof paper over the breast if it seems to be browning too quickly.
Alternatively, wrap the bird in foil before cooking, with the join along the top, or use a transparent roasting bag, following the instructions. Allow the same cooking time but open the foil for the final 15–20 minutes to allow

the bird to brown.
Serve with roast potatoes and green vegetables or a tossed green salad; also bacon rolls, chipolata sausages, bread sauce and thin gravy made from the giblets.
To roast a very small bird, spread with softened butter and put a knob of butter inside. Wrap in buttered paper and cook for only about ½–¾ hour, according to size. Remove the paper for the last 15 minutes to brown the breast.

Chicken with ginger

serves 6

3 × 15 ml spoons (3 tbsps) cooking
  oil
75 g (3 oz) butter
6 chicken joints
40 g (1½ oz) seasoned flour
3 medium-sized onions, skinned
  and sliced
10 ml spoon (2 level tsps)
  powdered ginger
15 ml spoon (1 level tbsp) French
  mustard
600 ml (1 pint) chicken stock
3 × 15 ml spoons (3 tbsps) medium
  sherry
salt and freshly ground black
  pepper
175 g (6 oz) button mushrooms,
  wiped and stalks removed

Heat the oil and half the butter in a frying pan. Toss the chicken

joints in seasoned flour to coat and fry until evenly browned. Drain from the fat and place in a large casserole. Reheat the fat, add the onions and fry. Stir in any excess flour, ginger and mustard; cook for a few minutes. Off the heat, stir in the stock and sherry. Bring to the boil, stirring. Adjust seasoning and pour over the chicken.
In a clean pan, melt the remaining butter and quickly sauté the mushrooms; add to the casserole. Cover and cook in the oven at 170°C (325°F) mark 3 for about 1½ hours. If necessary, strain off the juices and reduce a little by boiling; return to the chicken before serving.

Poulet à l'orange

serves 4

2 × 15 ml spoons (2 tbsps) cooking
  oil
4 chicken portions, halved
packet white sauce mix
300 ml (½ pint) milk
2 medium oranges
white grapes for garnish

Fry the chicken pieces in the oil until well browned. Remove from the pan and place in a 2.3 litre (4 pint) casserole. Make up the sauce according to directions on the packet, using the milk. Thinly pare the rind (free of all

Poulet à l'orange, coated in orange sauce and garnished with grapes

pith) from 1½ oranges and cut in thin strips. Add these to the sauce, together with the juice of 1 orange. Pour the sauce over the chicken, cover and cook in the oven at 190°C (375°F) mark 5 for about 45 minutes, or until the chicken is tender.

Cut the remaining orange in slices and use it for garnish along with the grapes.

One-crust chicken pie

serves 6

1½ kg (3 lb) oven-ready chicken
100 g (4 oz) lean streaky bacon, rinded and chopped
100 g (4 oz) onions, skinned and thinly sliced
100 g (4 oz) mushrooms, stalked and sliced
15 ml spoon (1 tbsp) chopped parsley
½ × 2.5 ml spoon (¼ level tsp) mixed dried herbs
salt and pepper
2 × 15 ml spoons (2 tbsps) water
150 g (5 oz) shortcrust pastry i.e. made with 150 g (5 oz) flour, etc
beaten egg to glaze

Skin the chicken, carve off all the flesh and cut into pieces. Layer the chicken, bacon, onions and mushrooms in a shallow oven-proof dish about 700–900 ml (1¼–1½ pint) capacity and 5 cm (2 in) deep. Sprinkle the layers with parsley, herbs and seasoning. Add the water.

Roll out the pastry and use to make a lid. Cut the pastry trimmings into leaves and use to decorate the top of the pie. Brush with the beaten egg. Cut a slit in the pastry lid, place on a baking sheet and cook in the oven at 180°C (350°F) mark 4 for about 1½ hours. Remove the pie from the oven and serve at once.

Poulet en cocotte

serves 4

For stuffing:
100 g (4 oz) sausage meat

2 × 15 ml spoons (2 level tbsps) fresh white breadcrumbs
1 chicken liver, chopped
2 × 15 ml spoons (2 tbsps) chopped parsley

1½–1¾ kg (3–3½ lb) oven-ready chicken
salt and freshly ground black pepper
65 g (2½ oz) butter
225 g (8 oz) lean back bacon, in one piece, rinded
½ kg (1 lb) potatoes, peeled
175 g (6 oz) shallots, skinned
½ kg (1 lb) small new carrots, scraped
chopped parsley to garnish

Mix together all the stuffing ingredients in a bowl until well blended. Adjust seasoning. Stuff the chicken at the neck end, plump up and secure with a

One-crust chicken pie is appetizing to look at and delicious to eat

skewer. Truss the bird as for roasting and season well with the salt and pepper.

Melt the butter in a large frying pan, add the chicken and fry, turning, until browned all over. Place the chicken and butter in a large casserole. Cut the bacon into 2 cm (¾ in) cubes, add to the casserole, cover and cook at 180°C (350°F) mark 4 for 15 minutes. Meanwhile, cut the potatoes into 2.5 cm (1 in) dice. Remove the casserole from the oven and baste the chicken. Surround with the potatoes, shallots and carrots, turning them in the fat. Season, return to the oven and cook for a further 1½ hours. Garnish with chopped parsley.

Have a hot plate to hand for carving the bird, but serve the vegetables and juices straight from the casserole.

Sautéed chicken with banana and lemon

serves 4

1½ kg (3 lb) roasting chicken
seasoned flour
100 g (4 oz) streaky bacon rashers
50 g (2 oz) butter
3 bananas
2 × 15 ml spoons (2 tbsps) lemon juice
chopped parsley

Skin the chicken and joint into 8 pieces. Discard rib carcass (use this for stock later). Toss each piece well in seasoned flour. Remove rind from the bacon and scissor-snip into small strips. Dry fry in a large pan until the fat runs.

Add the butter, then gently fry the chicken until golden brown on all sides. Cover and cook, turning occasionally, for about 45 minutes until thoroughly cooked and tender.

Skin and thickly slice bananas, add to chicken. Pour lemon juice over and cook for about 3 minutes until banana is soft but not mushy. Adjust seasoning. Sprinkle with chopped parsley and serve.

Simmered chicken with pasta

serves 4-6

½ kg (1 lb) cooked chicken meat, cut in strips
75 g (3 oz) butter
350 g (12 oz) onion, chopped
5 × 15 ml spoons (5 tbsps) flour
400 g (14 oz) can tomatoes
300 ml (½ pint) chicken stock
2 × 15 ml spoons (2 level tbsps) tomato paste
15 ml spoon (1 level tbsp) basil
2 cloves garlic, skinned and crushed
salt and pepper

Right: Sautéed chicken with banana and lemon

Serve Tandoori chicken as part of an Indian meal with traditional accompaniments

600 ml (1 pint) milk
1 carrot, 1 onion, 1 bay leaf
100 g (4 oz) lasagne sheets
50 g (2 oz) Parmesan cheese,
*   grated*

For the cold chicken, simmer a 1¾ kg (3½ lb) oven-ready bird in water with flavouring vegetables and seasoning for about 40 minutes.

Melt 50 g (2 oz) butter in a large pan and sauté onion until transparent. Stir in 2 × 15 ml spoons (2 level tbsps) flour. Cook 1 minute. Add tomatoes, their juices, stock, chicken, tomato paste, basil, garlic and seasonings. Bring to the boil. Simmer 10 minutes.

Bring milk to the boil with carrot, onion and bay leaf. Leave off heat for 10 minutes. Cook lasagne, drain well.

Melt remaining butter in a pan, stir in the remaining flour and make a sauce with the strained milk.

In a large buttered dish (about 2.6 litre (4½ pint)) layer up lasagne, chicken mixture and white sauce,

finishing with sauce. Sprinkle with Parmesan, bake at 200°C (400°F) mark 6 until brown and bubbling – about 30 minutes.

Tandoori chicken

serves 4

4 chicken joints
salt and pepper
150 g (5 oz) plain yoghurt
15 ml spoon (1 level tbsp) chilli
*   powder*
pinch of ground ginger
pinch of ground coriander
1 small clove garlic, skinned and
*   crushed*
juice of 1 small lemon
5 × 5 ml spoons (1½ tbsps) butter

Remove any protruding bones from the chicken joints, wipe and season with salt and pepper.

Combine the yoghurt with the chilli powder, ginger, coriander, garlic, lemon juice, 2.5 ml spoon (½ level tsp) black pepper and 5 ml spoon (1 level tsp) salt. Mix well and add the chicken pieces. Leave to stand for 3–4 hours, turning several times.

Remove the chicken from the marinade, shaking off as much of the liquid as possible, then pour a little melted butter over each chicken joint. Place the joints on the grill grid and brown quickly on both sides under a hot grill. Remove the chicken and place each joint on a piece of kitchen foil, about 38 cm (15 in) square. Fold over the sides of the foil, making a double join in the centre, and make a double fold in each end of the foil to seal. Place each packet in the grill pan, without grid, reduce heat to about half, and cook 20–30 minutes turning once during cooking time.

Heat the spicy marinade and serve separately.

Serve with poppadums and

melon and banana salad.

Roast chicken with pecan stuffing

serves 6

2 kg (4 lb) oven-ready chicken
melted butter or oil
salt and pepper

For stuffing:
heart and liver from the chicken
50 g (2 oz) fresh white
*   breadcrumbs*
50 g (2 oz) shelled pecans, chopped
*   (or 25 g (1 oz) shelled walnuts,*
*   chopped)*
1 egg, hard-boiled and chopped
pinch of ground nutmeg
pinch of ground mace
pinch of dried thyme

1 × 15 ml spoon (1 tbsp) chopped
  parsley
pinch of celery salt
50 g (2 oz) mushrooms, wiped and
  chopped
40 g (1½ oz) butter
1 small onion, skinned and
  chopped
2 × 15 ml spoons (2 tbsps) stock
freshly ground black pepper

Place the heart and liver in a small saucepan, cover with water, simmer for 10 minutes, drain, finely chop or mince and cool. Add this mixture to the breadcrumbs, nuts, egg, spices, herbs and celery salt in a bowl. Sauté the mushrooms in half the butter for 3–4 minutes and add to the other ingredients. Fry the onion in the remaining butter and add to the bowl with the stock. Season with pepper and mix well.
Wipe inside the chicken with a clean, damp cloth, stuff and truss. Brush with melted butter or oil and season.
Roast in the oven at 190°C (375°F) mark 5, allowing 20 minutes per ½ kg (lb), plus 20 minutes. Serve with roast potatoes, courgettes and gravy made with chicken stock.

Bird in a pan with parsley sauce

serves 6

1¾ kg (3½ lb) boiling fowl
900 ml (1½ pints) light stock,
  seasoned
½ lemon, sliced
a few parsley stalks
½ kg (1 lb) young carrots, scraped
6 small onions, skinned
50 g (2 oz) butter
50 g (2 oz) flour
15 ml spoon (1 tbsp) lemon juice
4 × 15 ml spoons (4 tbsps) chopped
  parsley
150 ml (¼ pint) milk
salt and freshly ground black
  pepper

Place the bird in a large saucepan with the stock, lemon slices and parsley stalks. Cover and simmer for 2½ hours. Turn two or three times during cooking.
Cut carrots in half lengthwise and add with the whole onions to the pan, cook for a further 30–45 minutes until tender.

Discard lemon and parsley.
Using a draining spoon lift the bird and vegetables on to a serving plate. Keep warm. Reduce liquor to 600 ml (1 pint) by fast boiling. Strain. Skim off surface fat. Melt butter in the saucepan, add flour, cook 1 minute. Add stock, stirring, and bring to the boil. Add lemon juice, parsley, milk. Adjust seasoning. Simmer 1–2 minutes. Use a little sauce to mask the chicken and vegetables. Serve the rest separately.

Chicken au gratin with pasta

serves 4-6

1¾ kg (3½ lb) oven-ready chicken
4 bacon rashers, rinded
100 g (4 oz) onion, sliced
100 g (4 oz) carrot, peeled and
  sliced
1 celery stalk, sliced
150 ml (¼ pint) chicken stock
1 bouquet garni
75 g (3 oz) butter
50 g (2 oz) flour
400 ml (¾ pint) milk
75 g (3 oz) Cheddar cheese, grated
3 × 15 ml spoons (3 tbsps)
  top-of-the-milk
salt and pepper
225 g (8 oz) pasta bows, freshly
  cooked
2 × 15 ml spoons (2 tbsps) chopped
  parsley
poppy seeds (optional)

Wipe chicken and portion into neat pieces. Scissor-snip bacon rashers into a large flameproof dish. Scatter onion, carrot and celery on top. Pour over seasoned stock, add chicken and bouquet garni. Cover and cook 5 mins. Transfer to the oven at 180°C (350°F) mark 4 for 1 hour. Remove chicken, keep warm. Strain off chicken juices and reduce to half. Remove bouquet garni and set bacon mixture aside. Melt 50 g (2 oz) butter, stir in flour, cook 1–2 minutes. Gradually add milk, stirring, then bring to the boil. Add reduced chicken juices. Add two thirds of cheese and simmer 1–2 minutes. Blend in top-of-the-milk and season. Fold remaining butter, parsley and poppy seeds into pasta. Place bacon mixture in the base of a serving dish, top with two-thirds of the pasta, then the chicken. Pour the sauce over, sprinkle with remaining cheese and brown under the grill. Serve rest of pasta separately.

A dish with Italian origin, Chicken au gratin with pasta makes a light supper served with salad

Blanquette of rabbit

serves 4-6

1 kg (2 lb) rabbit joints
175 g (6 oz) lean bacon, rinded and
*   diced*
1 large onion, skinned
1 clove
1 clove garlic, skinned and crushed
bouquet garni
salt and freshly ground black
*   pepper*
150 ml (¼ pint) white stock
15 ml spoon (1 tbsp) lemon juice
cold water
25 g (1 oz) margarine
2 × 15 ml spoons (2 level tbsps)
*   flour*
2 egg yolks
3 × 15 ml spoons (3 tbsps) cream
*   or top-of-the-milk*

For garnish:
small onions, sautéed
button mushrooms, sautéed
chopped parsley
small slices white bread, fried

Chop each joint in two. Put with the bacon, clove-studded onion, garlic, bouquet garni and seasoning in a large pan. Add the stock, lemon juice and enough water just to cover. Bring to the boil, skim, cover and simmer until the rabbit is really tender and leaving the bone – about 1½ hours. Strain off the liquid, discard the onion and bouquet garni.

Keep the rabbit warm in a clean casserole. Melt the fat, stir in the flour and cook for 2 minutes. Gradually add 600 ml (1 pint) of the cooking liquor, bring to the boil and simmer for 2–3 minutes,

Right: casserole of rabbit with juniper berries

stirring. Beat the egg yolks and cream together and slowly add the warm – not hot – stock. Adjust seasoning and re-heat, but do not boil. Pour the sauce over the rabbit and add the sautéed onions and mushrooms. Garnish with parsley and arrange triangles of fried bread around the edge.

Brown casserole of rabbit

serves 4

1 rabbit, jointed
50 g (2 oz) seasoned flour
50 g (2 oz) dripping
1 onion or leek, skinned and sliced
1 meat extract cube or 10 ml spoon
*   (2 level tsps) powdered meat*
*   extract*
600 ml (1 pint) stock or water
2 carrots, peeled and diced
1 celery stalk, scrubbed and
*   chopped*
bouquet garni
15 ml spoon (1 tbsp) tomato
*   ketchup*
pinch of ground nutmeg
fried croûtons to garnish

Soak the rabbit joints in cold salted water to remove the blood. Dry the pieces and toss in flour, then fry in the dripping, several joints at a time, until lightly browned. Remove from the pan, add the onion or leek and fry gently for a few minutes; add the

Brown casserole of rabbit can also be served with forcemeat balls

remaining flour and fry until lightly browned. Add the meat extract with the liquid and stir until boiling.

Put the rabbit and the vegetables into a casserole and pour the sauce over. Add the bouquet garni, ketchup and nutmeg, cover and cook in the centre of the oven at 180°C (350°F) mark 4 for about 2 hours. Remove the herbs, adjust seasoning and serve the casserole garnished with fried croûtons.

Casserole of rabbit with juniper berries

serves 6

corn oil
1¼ kg (2½ lb) rabbit pieces
4 × 15 ml spoons (4 level tbsps)
  flour
2 × 15 ml spoons (2 level tbsps)
  tomato paste
400 ml (¾ pint) rich brown stock
5 ml spoon (1 level tsp) dried fines
  herbes
2 bay leaves
5 ml spoon (1 level tsp) salt
freshly ground black pepper
8 juniper berries
1 clove garlic, skinned and crushed
225 g (8 oz) back bacon rashers,
  rinded
4 slices white bread

Heat 3 × 15 ml spoons (3 tbsps) oil and quickly brown the rabbit pieces. Place them in a large ovenproof casserole. Add the flour and tomato paste to the pan juice and cook for 1–2 minutes, then stir in the stock. Add the herbs and seasoning. Lightly crush the berries and add them to the pan with the garlic. Bring to the boil for 2 minutes, pour over rabbit, cover and cook in the centre of the oven at 170°C (325°F) mark 3 for 2–2½ hours or until tender. Stretch the bacon with the back of a knife. Halve the rashers and make into rolls. Thread the rolls on skewers and grill until crisp, take them off the skewers and stir into the casserole 30 minutes before the end of the cooking time. Trim the crusts from the bread and cut into triangles. Heat a little corn oil and fry the bread. Drain and serve separately.

Chicken bake

serves 4

175 g (6 oz) cooked chicken, diced
50 g (2 oz) margarine
2 medium onions, skinned and
  chopped
3 celery stalks, chopped
50 g (2 oz) peanuts
2 × 15 ml spoons (2 level tbsps)
  flour
300 ml (½ pint) milk
75 g (3 oz) Cheddar cheese, grated
small packet crisps, crushed

Place the chicken in a small casserole or pie dish. Melt the margarine and sauté the onion until transparent, then add the celery and peanuts and fry gently for 2–3 minutes. Sprinkle the flour into the pan; blend and cook for 1–2 minutes. Gradually stir in the milk and cook, stirring, until thick and smooth. Add half the cheese and stir to blend; pour over the chicken. Mix together the remaining cheese with the crushed crisps and sprinkle over the top. Bake at 200°C (400°F) mark 6, for about 30 minutes until crisp and golden. Serve with a tomato and cucumber salad.

Sweet-sour rabbit with prunes

serves 4

1 kg (2 lb) rabbit, jointed
175 g (6 oz) onions, skinned and
  sliced
300 ml (½ pint) dry cider
300 ml (½ pint) chicken stock
1 bay leaf
2 × 15 ml spoons (2 tbsps)
  redcurrant jelly
a few peppercorns
8 whole prunes, stoned
50 g (2 oz) seedless raisins
10 ml spoon (2 level tsps) cornflour
15 ml spoon (1 tbsp) malt vinegar
salt and freshly ground black
  pepper
chopped parsley
fried almonds

Marinate the rabbit overnight with the onion and cider. Discard the onion and place the cider and rabbit in a flameproof casserole; add the chicken stock, bay leaf, redcurrant jelly and a few peppercorns. Bring to the boil. Submerge the prunes and raisins in the liquid. Cover the casserole tightly and cook in the oven at 170°C (325°F) mark 3 for about 1½ hours, or until the rabbit is tender and the prunes plump. Remove meat and discard bones. Arrange the rabbit, prunes and raisins in a warm serving dish, add the cornflour blended with the vinegar to the sauce, adjust seasoning and boil 1–2 minutes. Pour over the rabbit and garnish with parsley and fried almonds.

Right: *Chicken bake – an excellent way of using leftover chicken*

Fish

food for thought

Fish and bacon casserole

serves 6

15 g (½ oz) butter
100 g (4 oz) bacon, rinded and
  chopped
3 onions, skinned and chopped
¾ kg (1½ lb) white fish, free of
  skin and bones
salt
cayenne pepper
5 ml spoon (1 tsp) Worcestershire
  sauce
150 ml (¼ pint) tomato sauce
150 ml (¼ pint) water

Fry the bacon and onion in the butter. Put alternate layers of bacon and onion and the fish into a casserole, sprinkling each layer with salt and very little cayenne. Mix the Worcestershire and tomato sauces with the water and pour over the fish. Cover and cook in the oven at 180°C (350°F) mark 4 for 45 minutes.

Fish cakes

serves 4

½ kg (1 lb) smoked haddock
¾ kg (1½ lb) potatoes, peeled and
  quartered
50 g (2 oz) butter
3 × 15 ml spoons (3 tbsps) chopped
  parsley
salt and pepper
milk or beaten egg to bind
1 or 2 eggs, beaten, to coat
dry breadcrumbs
fat for frying

Poach the fish in water until tender, drain, discard the skin and flake the flesh. Boil and drain the potatoes and mash with the butter. Mix the fish with the potato, parsley and salt and pepper to taste, binding if necessary with a little milk or egg. Form the mixture into a roll on a floured board, cut into 16 slices and shape into cakes. Coat with egg and crumbs. Fry in shallow fat until crisp and golden; drain well on absorbent kitchen paper.
Serve with tomato or parsley sauce.

Left: *Fish chowder*

Fish chowder

serves 6

3 rashers of lean bacon, rinded and chopped
1 large onion, skinned and sliced
700 g (1½ lb) fresh haddock, cooked and flaked
1½ × 400 g (14 oz) cans tomatoes
3 potatoes, peeled and diced
750 ml (1½ pints) fish stock
salt and freshly ground black pepper
1 bay leaf
3 cloves
175 ml (6 fl oz) milk
chopped parsley

Fry the bacon until the fat runs. Add the onion and fry until clear. Add the fish, tomatoes and potatoes, with the stock and seasonings, and simmer gently for about 30 minutes. Add the milk and remove the bay leaves and cloves, then reheat gently. Serve in bowls, with a little chopped parsley sprinkled on top.

Fish pilau

serves 4

Garam masala is a traditional Indian spice mixture consisting of ground cloves, powdered cinnamon, ground black pepper, cumin seeds and ground cardamom seeds

¾ kg (1½ lb) cod fillet
50 g (2 oz) ghee or butter
5 ml spoon (1 level tsp) powdered turmeric
2.5 ml spoon (½ level tsp) chilli powder
10 ml spoon (2 tsps) garam masala
10 ml spoon (2 tsps) lemon juice
2 onions, skinned and sliced
225 g (8 oz) long grain rice
1 litre (1¾ pints) water
2 bay leaves
tomatoes to garnish

Skin the fish, wipe it and cut into cubes. Melt half the ghee or butter and add the turmeric, chilli powder and garam masala; fry for 5 minutes and add the lemon juice. Cook the fish in this mixture for 10–15 minutes, then remove and place on a plate. Melt the remaining fat in a second pan and fry the onions until pale golden brown. Wash the rice in cold running water, drain thoroughly and add to the pan with the onions. Continue frying for 3–5 minutes. Add the gravy mixture from the first pan, with the water and bay leaves and cook for 20–30 minutes, by which time the liquid will be absorbed and the rice tender. Add the fish, stir gently and remove the bay leaves. Garnish with sliced tomato.

Fish pie

serves 4

¾ kg (1½ lb) potatoes
3 × 15 ml spoons (3 tbsps) milk
25 g (1 oz) butter
salt and pepper
½ kg (1 lb) cod fillet or any white fish including coley
300 ml (½ pint) milk
100 g (4 oz) frozen peas
40 g (1½ oz) butter or margarine
40 g (1½ oz) flour
50 g (2 oz) Cheddar cheese, grated
1 large tomato, cut into 8 pieces

Butter a 1.1 litre (2 pint) ovenproof dish. Peel and boil the potatoes in salted water until tender when tested with the point of a knife or fork. Drain and mash with a fork or potato masher (if the potatoes are to be piped press them through a sieve) and return to the pan. Add milk and 25 g (1 oz) butter and beat well with a wooden spoon. Season and keep warm.

Wipe the fish, cut it into 2 pieces and place them in a saucepan with 150 ml (¼ pint) water and the milk. Bring the liquid to the boil, reduce the heat until the fish is cooking only gently. Cover and leave for about 10 minutes to continue to cook, until the fish flakes easily. Drain off the liquid and keep it on one side.

Discard the skin from the fish and coarsely flake the flesh. Turn into the pie dish with the frozen peas. Melt 40 g (1½ oz) butter, stir in the flour and cook until the mixture bubbles. Remove from the heat and gradually beat in 400 ml (¾ pint) liquid used to cook the fish. Return the pan to the heat and bring to the boil, stirring all the time until the sauce thickens. This will take about 2 minutes. Add the cheese and stir until melted; season. Pour the sauce over the fish.

Pile the creamy potato round the edge of the dish to make a collar or spoon it into a fabric forcing bag fitted with a large star vegetable nozzle and pipe it round, as in our picture. Bake at the top of the oven at 220°C (425°F) mark 7 until the potato is golden – about 25–30 minutes. Garnish with tomato.

Herrings braised in wine

serves 6

½ bottle red wine
thick slices of onion, carrot and celery
1 bay leaf
bouquet garni
6 peppercorns
salt and pepper
6 herrings (or other small oily fish), cleaned
sautéed button mushrooms, small onions and parsley

Place the wine, sliced vegetables, herbs, peppercorns and seasoning in a saucepan. Cover and simmer for 30 minutes.

Arrange the herrings in a single layer in an ovenproof dish. Strain the liquor over them, adding a little water, if necessary, almost to cover them. Cover and cook at 170°C (325°F) mark 3 for 1 hour. Garnish with sautéed mushrooms, small onions and parsley.

Fish pie with piped potatoes, browned in the oven, for garnish

Fish puffs

serves 4

½ kg (1 lb) potatoes, peeled
½ kg (1 lb) white fish
1 small onion, grated
2 × 10 ml spoons (4 level tsps)
  curry powder
salt and pepper
50 g (2 oz) butter, melted
4 eggs, beaten
oil for deep-frying

Boil and drain the potatoes and mash them. Poach and flake the fish, mix it with the potatoes and remaining ingredients (except the oil for frying) and beat until smooth.

Heat the oil until it will brown a cube of bread in 40 seconds. Drop the fish mixture into it with a teaspoon, fry quickly until golden, drain on crumpled kitchen paper and serve with a well-flavoured sauce, such as tomato or tartare.

Fish ramekins

serves 6

150 ml (¼ pint) single cream
275 g (10 oz) can pilchards in
  tomato sauce
3 × 15 ml spoons (3 tbsps) lemon
  juice
salt and pepper
6 large eggs

Spoon 15 ml spoon (1 tbsp) of cream into each of 6 ramekin dishes. Mash the pilchards and divide between the dishes and sprinkle with lemon juice. Season to taste. Break an egg into each dish and top with remaining cream. Bake at 180°C (350°F) mark 4 for 15 minutes until the egg is set. Serve at once with Melba toast.

Crisply fried Fish puffs make an ideal first course

Cider and haddock casserole

serves 4-6

½–¾ kg (1–1½ lb) haddock or cod
    fillets, skinned
¼ kg (½ lb) tomatoes, skinned and
    sliced
50 g (2 oz) button mushrooms,
    sliced
15 ml spoon (1 tbsp) chopped
    parsley
salt and freshly ground black
    pepper
150 ml (¼ pint) cider
2 × 15 ml spoons (2 tbsps) fresh
    white breadcrumbs
2 × 15 ml spoons (2 tbsps) grated
    cheese

Wipe the fish, cut into cubes and
lay these in an ovenproof dish.
Cover with the sliced tomatoes
and mushrooms, the parsley and
seasonings and pour the cider
over. Cover with foil and cook in
the centre of the oven at 180°C
(350°F) mark 4, for 20–25
minutes. Sprinkle with the
breadcrumbs and cheese and
brown in oven, 220°C (425°F)
mark 7, or under a hot grill.

Cider and haddock casserole makes a pleasant change

removing any bones, and add to
the sauce with the chopped parsley, salt and pepper. Bring to the
boil.
Pour into individual serving
dishes and garnish each with
wedges of hard-boiled egg.

Make up the white sauce by using
all milk or half milk and half fish
stock. Blend the mustard, sugar
and vinegar to a smooth cream
and stir into the sauce.
Serve the herrings hot, with the
mustard sauce.

50 g (2 oz) butter
2 eating apples
juice of ½ lemon
pepper
chopped parsley

Bone the fish and cut in halves
down the centre. Dip fillets in
seasoned flour and fry in the oil
and 25 g (1 oz) butter until crisp
and golden on each side; keep
warm. Wipe pan out with absorbent kitchen paper.
Peel and core the apples and cut
each into 8 pieces, then add the
rest of the butter to the pan and
sauté the apple until tender but
still in whole pieces. Add the
lemon juice and a dusting of
freshly ground pepper (with a
little more butter if needed).
Arrange the fillets in a dish, overlapping each other, spoon the
apple mixture over and sprinkle
with chopped parsley.

Herrings with lemon crumble

serves 4

4 herrings
4 × 15 ml spoons (4 tbsps) cooking
    oil
4 × 1 cm (½ in) slices day-old
    bread
50 g (2 oz) butter
grated rind and juice of 1 lemon
4 × 15 ml spoons (4 tbsps) chopped
    parsley
lemon wedges

Clean the herrings, cut off the
heads and fins, but leave on the
tails. Brush the fish with oil. Grill
for 8 minutes under a medium
heat, turning once.
Crumb the bread. Melt the butter

Finnan haddie

serves 4

2 Finnan haddock (or smoked cod
    fillets) total weight approx. ¼ kg
    (1½ lb)
600 ml (1 pint) milk
50 g (2 oz) butter
50 g (2 oz) flour
chopped parsley
salt and pepper
2 eggs, hard-boiled

Place the fish skin side up under a
hot grill for a few minutes – this
makes skinning very simple. Peel
the skin off and cut the fish into 8
pieces. Poach in milk for about 15
minutes until tender. Drain off
the milk into a measure and make
up to 600 ml (1 pint) with more
milk if necessary.
Melt the butter in a pan, stir in the
flour and gradually blend in the
measured milk. Flake the fish,

Grilled herrings with mustard sauce

serves 4

4 herrings
300 ml (½ pint) white sauce
15 ml spoon (1 level tbsp) dry
    mustard
10 ml spoon (2 level tsps) sugar
15 ml spoon (1 tbsp) vinegar

Have the heads cut off and the
fish gutted but left whole.
Wash and wipe them and make
2–3 diagonal cuts in the flesh on
both sides of the fish and sprinkle
with salt and pepper. Brush with
oil or melted butter and cook on a
greased grill grid for 10–15
minutes under a moderate heat,
turning the fish once, until
thoroughly cooked on both sides.

Herring fillets Normandy-style

serves 4

4 herrings (or ½ kg (1 lb) oily fish)
seasoned flour
2 × 15 ml spoons (2 tbsps) oil

Herring fillets Normandy-style – cheap and quick to prepare

Goujons of whiting make a superb first course

peppercorns and salt. In a saucepan, bring the vinegar, water and lemon juice to the boil. Pour over the fish. Bake, uncovered, in the centre of the oven at 170°C (325°F) mark 3 for 25–30 minutes. Baste the mackerel 2 or 3 times with the marinade during the cooking. When cooked, allow the fish to cool at room temperature. Cover with foil and marinate in the refrigerator for at least 6 hours.

Carefully lift the fish from the liquid and transfer to a serving platter. Garnish with lemon slices and parsley.

Fried fillets of mackerel

serves 4

4 mackerel, filleted
oil for frying
a few button mushrooms, wiped
2 onions, skinned and thinly sliced
2 small cloves garlic, skinned and crushed
4 × 15 ml spoons (4 tbsps) vinegar
grilled tomatoes
parsley, chopped

Fry the fillets quickly in very hot shallow oil, then arrange them on a dish and keep hot. Cook the mushrooms, onion and garlic in the reheated oil, browning them well, and spoon over the fillets. Heat the vinegar until very hot, pour over the fillets and surround with grilled tomatoes. Sprinkle with chopped parsley.

---

in a small saucepan, stir in the breadcrumbs and cook over medium heat until golden brown. Remove from the heat and add the lemon rind, juice and parsley. Put the breadcrumb mixture in a serving dish and place the herrings on top. Garnish with lemon.

Fish provençale

serves 4

¾ kg (1½ lb) white fish
100 g (4 oz) butter
salt and pepper
2 onions, skinned and chopped
1 green or red pepper, seeded and chopped
2 × 15 ml spoons (2 level tbsps) tomato paste
2 × 15 ml spoons (2 level tbsps) flour
425 g (15 oz) can peeled tomatoes
dash of Worcestershire sauce
5 ml spoon (1 level tsp) sugar
1 pkt. instant potato (or 450 g

(1 lb) potatoes, boiled and creamed)
approx. 6 × 15 ml spoons (6 tbsps) milk

Cut the fish into 4 pieces and place in a buttered grill pan, dot with butter and season. Grill for approximately 12 minutes, turning once and seasoning the second side when you turn it.

Melt half the butter in a saucepan. Fry the onion for 2–3 minutes, add the pepper and continue to fry gently for a further 3–4 minutes. Stir the tomato paste and flour into the onion mixture, then the tomatoes. Bring to the boil, stirring all the time. Add a dash of Worcestershire sauce and the sugar. Continue to simmer.

Make up the instant potato, season and beat in the remaining butter, or beat the butter into creamed potatoes. If too solid, add a little milk. Spoon into a forcing bag fitted with a star nozzle. Pipe round edge of dish. Arrange the fish in the centre of the potato border. Stir the sauce well and spoon it carefully over the fish. Reheat under the grill for 1 minute.

Soused mackerel

serves 5

5 mackerel
50 g (2 oz) onion, skinned and sliced
sprigs of parsley
2 bay leaves
pinch dried thyme
12 whole peppercorns
2.5 ml spoon (½ level tsp) salt
175 ml (6 fl oz) white wine vinegar
175 ml (6 fl oz) water
2 × 15 ml spoons (2 tbsps) lemon juice
lemon slices and parsley for garnish

Remove the heads and gut the fish. Wash under cold running water and pat dry with absorbent kitchen paper. Lay the fish top to tail and side by side, in a shallow flameproof dish just big enough to hold them. Divide the onion slices into rings and arrange between and over the fish. Add the parsley sprigs, bay leaves, thyme,

Whiting pie

serves 3-4

½ kg (1 lb) whiting, filleted
300 ml (½ pint) milk
1 small onion, skinned
1 bay leaf
a few peppercorns
100 g (4 oz) bacon rashers, rinded
creamy mashed potato (for topping)

For the sauce:
5 ml spoon (1 level tsp) made mustard
2.5 ml spoon (½ level tsp) ground nutmeg

Right: Fried fillets of mackerel

Poach the whiting in the milk together with the onion, bay leaf and peppercorns, for 20 minutes. Meanwhile grill the bacon until crisp, then crumble.

Make up 300 ml (½ pint) white sauce adding plenty of parsley; use the strained liquor from the fish. Add the mustard and nutmeg. Add the skinned, flaked fish together with the crumbled bacon. Turn into a pie-dish and top with potato. Cook until golden at 200°C (400°F) mark 6 for about ¾ hour.

Goujons of whiting

serves 4

½ kg (1 lb) boned and skinned
  whiting
15 g (½ oz) flour
1 large egg
salt and pepper
75 g (3 oz) bought golden
  breadcrumbs
oil for deep-frying

With a sharp knife, cut the whiting into strips about 2.5 cm (1 in) wide and 5 cm (2 in) long. Sift the flour on to one plate, whisk the egg, salt and pepper on another and put the breadcrumbs on a final plate. Coat the fish in the flour, shake well; dip into the egg and allow excess to drip off. Finally coat in the breadcrumbs. Deep-fry in oil a few pieces at a time at 182°C (360°F) for about 5 minutes. Drain well on absorbent paper; sprinkle with salt.

Arrange on a serving plate and serve with lemon twists.

Brandade provençale

serves 4

¾ kg (1½ lb) salt cod, cod fillet or
  other white fish
150 ml (¼ pint) olive oil
2 cloves of garlic, skinned and
  crushed
150 ml (¼ pint) milk
salt and pepper
grated nutmeg

juice of 1 lemon
1 lemon, quartered
1 egg, hard-boiled and sliced
toasted croûtons

Soak salt fish overnight, then drain. Place the fish in fresh cold water, bring to the boil and simmer for 5 minutes. Drain the fish, remove any skin and bones and return the flesh to the saucepan. In a second pan, heat the oil and add the garlic (do not have the oil so hot that it will brown the garlic). Heat the milk in a third pan but do not boil it. Using a wooden spoon, mash the fish and add alternate spoonfuls of warm milk and warm oil, stirring constantly over the heat until all the oil and milk have been used up and the fish is a thick purée.

Season and add the nutmeg and lemon juice. Turn into a hot serving dish and garnish with lemon quarters, slices of hard-boiled egg and croûtons.

Sprats on skewers

Wash the sprats and dry them thoroughly, then toss in seasoned flour. Take some small skewers and thread 6–8 sprats on each, sticking the skewers through the heads and pushing the sprats close together. Fry in hot fat, turning them when browned on the underside. Drain on paper. Garnish with wedges of lemon.

Plaki

serves 4

6 onions, skinned and finely
  chopped
olive oil
chopped parsley
4 tomatoes, skinned and sliced, or
  a little tomato sauce (fresh or
  bottled)
salt and pepper
1 kg (2 lb) fish, filleted (white or
  oily fish, as available)
1 tomato for garnish
1 lemon for garnish

Fry the onions in a little oil and add the chopped parsley. When the onions are cooked but not

brown, add the tomatoes and fry a little longer, or add the tomato sauce. Season.

Lay the fish in a greased oven-proof dish, pour the onion mixture over and bake in the oven at 220°C (425°F) mark 7 for about 15 minutes.

Garnish with slices of tomato and lemon.

Rollmops

serves 4

4 small salted herrings
4 onions, skinned and thinly sliced
finely chopped dill
bay leaves
cloves
allspice
mustard seeds
300 ml (½ pint) salad oil
300 ml (½ pint) vinegar
sugar to taste

Clean well and fillet the herrings, or ask the fishmonger to do this for you. Soak the fillets for about 10 hours in fresh cold water, then wipe dry on absorbent kitchen paper. Place a few slices of onion on each fillet, and a little chopped dill; roll up the fillets and secure with a cocktail stick. Place a layer of fillets in the bottom of a bowl or jar and scatter bay leaves, cloves, allspice and mustard seeds on top; repeat in alternate layers of herrings and spices.

Place the vinegar and oil in a pan and bring to the boil; add a little sugar to taste. When the liquid has cooled slightly, pour it over the herrings. Leave to marinate for 2–3 days before serving.

Tunafish creams

serves 6

200 ml (7 fl oz) sour cream
2 × 15 ml spoons (2 tbsps)
 mayonnaise
salt and pepper
dash of Worcestershire sauce
3 × 2.5 ml spoons (1½ tsps)
 chopped chives
10 ml spoon (2 tsps) capers,
 chopped
2.5 ml spoon (½ level tsp) finely
 grated onion

10 ml spoon (2 level tsps)
 powdered gelatine
2 × 15 ml spoons (2 tbsps) water
200 g (7 oz) can tuna steak,
 drained and flaked
2 eggs, hard-boiled and chopped
2 firm tomatoes for garnish
parsley

Combine the sour cream, mayonnaise, seasonings, herbs and onion. Dissolve the gelatine in the water in a basin over a pan of hot water. Cool slightly and stir into the cream mixture; add the tuna steak and eggs and mix well. Spoon into individual soufflé dishes and chill until set. To serve, garnish with tomato wedges and parsley.

Grilling fish

Most fish can be grilled, though the drier types are better cooked in other ways. The fish should be seasoned, sprinkled with lemon juice and (except for oily fish such as herrings) brushed liberally with melted butter. Cutlets should be tied neatly into shape. Fillets and large fish should be cooked in the grill pan rather than on the grid.

Cutlets and fillets: Grill first on one side for 3–10 minutes, depending on thickness, then turn with a flat, metal draining slice. Brush with fat and grill the second side. Serve very hot garnished with grilled tomato halves or parsley sprigs and a sauce.

Whole fish: Wash and scale the fish. Score it with a sharp knife in 3–4 places on each side (this allows the heat to penetrate the thick flesh more quickly), season and brush with melted butter if required. Line the pan with foil if you wish, to catch the juices, place the fish on the grid or in the pan and grill rather slowly, so that the flesh cooks thoroughly without the outside burning.

Turn the fish once or twice, handling it carefully to prevent breaking. To test whether the fish is done, insert the back of a knife next to the bone to see if the flesh comes away easily. Serve with maître d'hôtel butter or melted butter, lemon wedges and chopped parsley.

Left: Sprats on skewers and Rollmops – two delicious appetizers

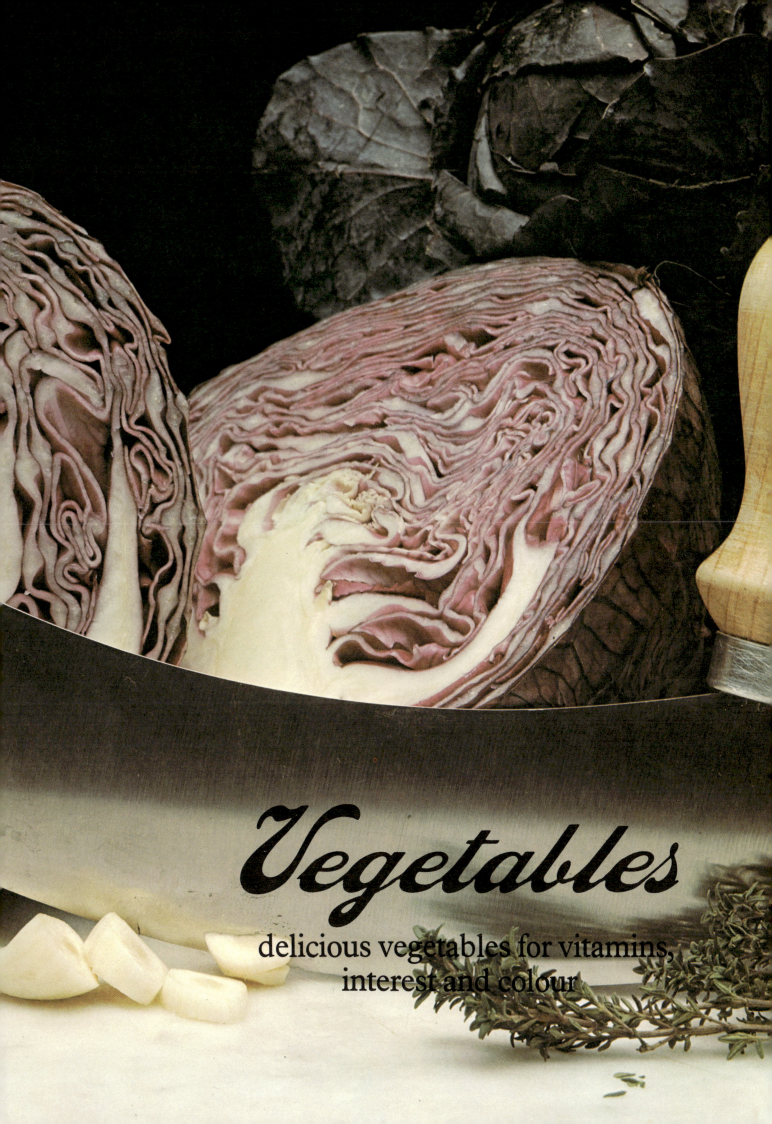

Vegetables

delicious vegetables for vitamins,
interest and colour

Chipped potatoes

allow 175–225 g (6–8 oz) potatoes per person

Peel the potatoes and cut into 0.5–1 cm (¼–½ in) slices, then into strips 0.5–1 cm (¼–½ in) wide. (For speed, several slices can be put on top of one another and cut together, or use a special 'chipper'). Place in cold water and leave for at least ½ hour; drain well and dry with a cloth. Heat oil in a deep fat fryer until one chip rises to the surface straight away, when dropped in the oil, surrounded by bubbles.

Put enough chips into the basket to about quarter-fill it and lower carefully into the fat. Cook for 6–7 minutes, remove and drain on absorbent paper. Repeat this procedure until all the chips have been cooked.

Just before serving, reheat the fat, test to make sure it is hot enough and fry the chips rapidly for about 3 minutes, until crisp and brown. Drain well on absorbent paper and serve at once in an uncovered dish, sprinkled with salt.

Note: *The initial soaking helps to remove the excess starch from the potatoes, making the chips crisp.*

Lyonnaise potatoes

serves 4

225 g (½ lb) onions, skinned and sliced
2 × 15 ml spoons (2 tbsps) cooking oil
½ kg (1 lb) sauté potatoes
chopped parsley

Fry the onions slowly in the oil until golden brown – about 10 minutes.

Serve in layers with the potatoes and sprinkle with chopped parsley.

Potato and bacon pan fry

serves 3

225 g (8 oz) streaky bacon
½ kg (1 lb) potatoes, peeled and very thinly sliced
100 g (4 oz) onion, skinned and thinly sliced
150 g (5 oz) Port Salut cheese
5 ml spoon (1 level tsp) dried fennel seed
salt and freshly ground black pepper

Remove rind and cut bacon into small pieces. Fry in a large – about 30.5 cm (12 in) – frying pan, until the fat runs and the bacon is golden and crispy.

Add the potato and onion to the pan. Remove rind from Port Salut, chop cheese into small pieces and add to the pan with the fennel. Stir and season. Cook over a fairly high heat until golden brown and crisp on the bottom. Place under a hot grill and cook until brown and crisp on top. Cut into 3 and serve.

Petits pois à la française

serves 4

¼ of a lettuce, washed and finely shredded
6 spring onions, halved and trimmed
a little parsley and mint, tied together
¾ kg (1½ lb) peas, shelled
150 ml (¼ pint) water
25 g (1 oz) butter
salt and pepper
10 ml spoon (2 level tsps) sugar
butter for serving

Put all the ingredients except the extra butter in a pan, cover closely and simmer until cooked – about 20–30 minutes.

Remove the parsley and mint, drain the peas well and serve with a knob of butter.

From left to right: *Glazed beetroots, Petits pois à la française and Lyonnaise potatoes*

Lyonnaise peas

serves 4

50 g (2 oz) butter
2 large onions, skinned and finely
  sliced
½ kg (1 lb) frozen peas
salt

Melt the butter in a small pan, add the onion and cook over gentle heat for 3 minutes. Meanwhile, bring a pan of salted water to the boil, add the peas and cook for 3 minutes. Drain the peas and mix with the onion.

Maître d'hôtel potatoes

serves 4

½ kg (1 lb) potatoes
15 ml spoon (1 tbsp) olive oil
salt and pepper
chopped parsley
15 ml spoon (1 tbsp) vinegar

Boil the potatoes in their skins and peel the potatoes while still warm. Cut into 0.5 cm (¼ in) slices. Heat the oil in a frying-pan, add the rest of the ingredients and toss the sliced potatoes in the mixture until well heated. Serve at once.

Sauté of peas

serves 4

few spring onions, trimmed
25 g (1 oz) butter
1 kg (1 lb) peas, shelled
salt and pepper
300 ml (½ pint) white stock
5 ml spoon (1 tsp) chopped parsley

Lightly fry the onions in the butter for about 2 minutes, then add the peas, salt and pepper and just enough stock to cover the peas. Cover with a tightly fitting lid and cook gently for 15–20 minutes, until the peas are tender: remove the lid after 10–15 minutes to allow the cooking liquid to evaporate. Sprinkle with parsley.

Above: *Potato and bacon pan fry*, below: *Baked tomatoes*

Carrots Cowan

serves 4

½ kg (1 lb) carrots
salt
15 g (½ oz) butter
2 × 15 ml spoons (2 tbsps) brown sugar
juice of 1 orange

Trim and scrape the carrots. Slice thinly if old, leave whole if young. Simmer in salted water for about 15 minutes, until cooked. Drain and add a knob of butter, the sugar and orange juice. Heat gently to melt the butter and dissolve the sugar, then simmer for 5 minutes.

Carrots Vichy

serves 4

½ kg (1 lb) carrots
75 g (3 oz) butter
15 ml spoon (1 tbsp) water
15 ml spoon (1 level tbsp) sugar
salt
chopped parsley

Scrub and scrape the carrots, then cut into thin julienne strips or slices. Melt the butter in a pan and add the water, sugar and carrots. Cover tightly and cook gently for ¾–1 hour, turning the carrots carefully from time to time. Sprinkle with a little salt and chopped parsley just before serving.

Glazed carrots

serves 4

50 g (2 oz) butter
½ kg (1 lb) whole young carrots
3 lumps sugar
½ × 2.5 ml spoon (¼ level tsp) salt
a little stock
chopped parsley

Melt the butter and add carrots, sugar, salt and enough stock to come half-way up carrots. Cook gently, uncovered, until soft. Remove carrots and boil liquid to reduce to a glaze. Return carrots and toss in glaze. Sprinkle with parsley.

Baked tomatoes

serves 4

8 large, firm tomatoes
25 g (1 oz) butter
50 g (2 oz) long grain rice
salt and pepper
50 g (2 oz) frozen peas, cooked

Cut a thin slice from the rounded end of each tomato, scoop out a little of the seed and core. Put a knob of butter in each and bake in the oven at 180°C (350°F) mark 4 for about 10 minutes. Meanwhile cook the rice for about 12 minutes in boiling, salted water and drain. Season the rice, spoon into the tomatoes and top with peas.

Tuna-filled tomatoes

serves 4

4 large tomatoes
50 g (2 oz) butter
1 onion, skinned and chopped
100 g (4 oz) button mushrooms, wiped and sliced
200 g (7 oz) can tuna, drained and flaked
2 × 15 ml spoons (2 tbsps) chopped parsley

Remove the top from each tomato, cutting in a zig-zag fashion with a small, sharp-pointed knife. Using a teaspoon, scoop out the soft core and seeds and discard. Put the tomato cases on a baking sheet.
Heat the butter in a frying pan, add the onion and cook until soft, without colouring. Add the mushrooms, continue cooking for a few minutes. Add the flaked tuna, together with the parsley. Mix well together and divide the filling between the tomatoes. Cover with kitchen foil and bake in the centre of the oven at 180°C (350°F) mark 4 for 20–30 minutes.

Baked stuffed onions

serves 4

4 medium-sized onions, skinned
2 × 15 ml spoons (2 level tbsps) fresh white breadcrumbs
salt and pepper
50 g (2 oz) cheese, grated
butter

Cook the onions in boiling salted water for 15–20 minutes, removing them before they are quite soft; drain and cool. Scoop out the centres, using a pointed knife to cut the onion top and a small spoon to remove the centres.
Chop the centres finely, mix with the crumbs, seasoning and 25 g (1 oz) cheese. Fill the onions and place them in a greased ovenproof dish. Put small knobs of butter on top and sprinkle with the remaining cheese. Bake in the centre of the oven at 200°C (400°F) mark 6 for 20–30 minutes, till the onions are cooked and browned.
Serve with tomato sauce.

Crisp fried onion rings

serves 4

4 large onions, skinned and cut into 0.5 cm (¼ in) slices
a little milk
a little flour
salt and pepper
oil for deep-frying

Separate the onion slices into rings and dip in the milk and then the seasoned flour. Heat the oil so that when one ring is dropped in, it rises to the surface surrounded by bubbles. Gradually add the rest of the rings to the oil and fry for 2–3 minutes until golden brown. Drain on crumpled absorbent kitchen paper, season and serve at once.

Dahl

serves 4

100 g (4 oz) red lentils
300 ml (½ pint) cold water
salt and pepper
1 onion, skinned and finely chopped
fat for frying
25 g (1 oz) butter or dripping

Wash the lentils and add to the water in a pan. Season and cook steadily for 1–1½ hours, adding more water if necessary. When tender, remove from heat and stir vigorously. Fry the onion; add to the lentils with the butter or dripping and stir over the heat to blend well.

Haricots verts aux tomates

serves 4

½ kg (1 lb) French beans
¼ kg (½ lb) firm tomatoes
40 g (1½ oz) butter
1 bay leaf
sprig of thyme
salt and pepper

Baked stuffed onions – onions filled with a savoury breadcrumb and cheese mixture

Sautéed Courgettes with tomatoes, finished au gratin

Top, tail and wash the beans, plunge into boiling salted water, cover and cook for 5 minutes. Scald the tomatoes and remove the skins, then quarter them. Drain the beans in a colander, melt the butter in the pan over gentle heat and return the beans, with the tomatoes, bay leaf and thyme. Season with salt and freshly ground black pepper. Cover with a tightly fitting lid; if the lid is rather loose, place a buttered round of greaseproof paper under it to hold it tight. Simmer gently for about 15 minutes, shaking the pan occasionally. Remove bay leaf and thyme before serving.

Glazed beetroots

serves 4

12 small beetroots, cooked
25 g (1 oz) butter
5 ml spoon (1 level tsp) sugar
salt and pepper
grated rind of 1 lemon

5 ml spoon (1 tsp) chopped chives
10 ml spoon (2 tsps) chopped parsley
juice of ½ lemon
15 ml spoon (1 tbsp) capers

Remove the skin, stalks and root ends from the beetroots. Melt the butter in a saucepan and add the beetroots, sugar, salt, pepper and lemon rind. Toss the beetroots in the pan over a medium heat until they are well coated; add the remaining ingredients, heat through and serve.

Sweet-sour red cabbage

serves 4

1 kg (2 lb) red cabbage, shredded
2 medium onions, skinned and sliced
2 cooking apples, peeled and chopped
10 ml spoon (2 level tsps) sugar
salt and pepper
bouquet garni

2 × 15 ml spoons (2 tbsps) water
2 × 15 ml spoons (2 tbsps) red wine vinegar
25 g (1 oz) butter or margarine

In a casserole, layer the cabbage with the onions, apples, sugar and seasoning. Put the bouquet garni in the centre.

Pour the water and vinegar over the mixture, cover tightly and cook at 150°C (300°F) mark 2 for about 2½ hours.

Just before serving, add the butter and mix well into the other ingredients.

Courgettes with tomatoes

serves 4

½ kg (1 lb) courgettes, cut into 0.5 cm (¼ in) slices
salt
65 g (2½ oz) butter
¼ kg (½ lb) tomatoes, skinned and chopped
15 ml spoon (1 tbsp) chopped parsley
1 small clove garlic, skinned and crushed
pepper
2.5 ml spoon (½ level tsp) sugar
50 g (2 oz) cheese, grated
25 g (1 oz) fresh white breadcrumbs

Put the courgette slices into a colander, sprinkle with salt and allow to drain for about an hour. Rinse and dry. Melt 50 g (2 oz) butter in a frying pan and put in the courgettes. Cook gently until soft and slightly transparent and put them in an ovenproof dish. Melt the remaining 15 g (½ oz) butter and cook the tomatoes, parsley, garlic, pepper and sugar together, stirring, until a thickish purée forms.

Re-season the mixture if necessary and pour it over the courgettes. Sprinkle with the cheese and breadcrumbs and grill until golden brown.

Dressed leeks

serves 6

½ kg (1 lb) leeks
3 × 15 ml spoons (3 tbsps) salad oil
15 ml spoon (1 tbsp) cider vinegar

Sweet-sour red cabbage – a delicious vegetable cooked in an unusual way

Variety rice served with Pork chop braise (page 30)

Season and stir in the lemon juice and chopped parsley. Spoon into individual dishes to serve.
Serve the mushrooms with hot toast fingers.

Braised celery

serves 4

4 small heads of celery, trimmed
  and scrubbed
50 g (2 oz) butter
stock
salt and pepper

Tie each head of celery securely to hold the shape. Fry lightly in 40 g (1½ oz) butter for 5 minutes until golden brown. Put in an ovenproof dish, add enough stock to come half-way up the celery, sprinkle with salt and pepper and add the remaining butter. Cover and cook in the centre of the oven at 180°C (350°F) Mark 4 for 1–1½ hours.
Remove the string and serve with the cooking liquid poured over.

2.5 ml spoon (½ level tsp) French
  mustard
15 g (½ oz) finely chopped onion
5 ml spoon (1 level tsp) caster
  sugar
salt and freshly ground black
  pepper

Trim about half the green part from the leeks. Cut the remainder of the leeks into 0.3 cm (⅛ in) slices and wash thoroughly in cold water. Drain, blanch in boiling salted water for 3–4 minutes, then cool quickly with cold water. Drain well.
Shake the remaining ingredients together in a screw-top jar, pour over the leeks and toss together.

Variety rice

serves 4

175 g (6 oz) long grain rice
salt
40 g (1½ oz) frozen peas
40 g (1½ oz) frozen sweet corn
  kernels

freshly ground black pepper

Cook the rice in boiling salted water for about 12 minutes, or until tender. Meanwhile cook the frozen vegetables according to the directions on the packets. Mix the rice and vegetables well together and season with pepper.

Jade spinach

serves 4

½ kg (1 lb) leaf spinach
6 × 15 ml spoons (6 tbsps) corn oil
150 ml (¼ pint) chicken stock
salt
lemon juice

Remove the coarse stems from the spinach. Wash thoroughly and drain. Heat the oil, add spinach, stock, seasoning and lemon juice.
Cook over a high heat for 20 seconds. Strain off the stock and put spinach in a serving dish.
Serve hot.

Champignons Marie

serves 4

350 g (12 oz) button mushrooms,
  wiped and stalks removed
3 × 15 ml spoons (3 tbsps) cooking
  oil
2 shallots, skinned and finely
  chopped
2 × 15 ml spoons (2 level tbsps)
  fine, dry breadcrumbs
salt and pepper
15 ml spoon (1 tbsp) lemon juice
2 × 15 ml spoons (2 tbsps) chopped
  parsley

Quarter the mushroom caps and half of the stalks. Heat the oil in a thick frying pan and fry them for 10 minutes, until brown. Chop the remaining stalks finely, mix with the chopped shallots and add to the mushrooms in the pan. Fry for a further 2–3 minutes. Drain any excess fat from the pan and add the breadcrumbs. Stir over gentle heat.

Pan Hagerty

serves 4

25 g (1 oz) dripping
½ kg (1 lb) potatoes, peeled and
  thinly sliced
225 g (8 oz) onions, peeled and
  thinly sliced
100 g (4 oz) Cheddar cheese,
  grated
salt and freshly ground black
  pepper

In a 20 cm (8 in) shallow frying pan, melt the dripping and gently swirl around the edges. Layer the potatoes, onions and grated cheese alternately in the pan, seasoning well between each layer. Finish with grated cheese on top and overlap potatoes round the edge. Cover with a lid, then let the contents fry gently for about 30 minutes until the onions and potatoes are nearly cooked. Remove the lid and brown the top under a hot grill.
Pan Hagerty should be served straight from the pan.

Salads

fresh and unusual salads

Cucumber salad

serves 4

½ cucumber (or 1 small ridge
  cucumber)
salt
4 × 10 ml spoons (2½ tbsps) salad
  oil
15 ml spoon (1 tbsp) wine vinegar
½ small onion, skinned and thinly
  sliced
paprika (optional)
freshly ground black pepper
  (optional)
15 ml spoon (1 tbsp) sour cream
  (optional)

Peel the cucumber and slice very
thinly. Place in a bowl, sprinkle
with salt and leave to stand for 1
hour. Rinse and squeeze in a
cloth to extract the surplus mois-
ture.
Pour over the oil and vinegar, mix
well and add the sliced onion.
Sprinkle with paprika or black
pepper, or spoon over the sour
cream.

Leek and tomato salad

serves 4

2 young tender leeks, washed
2 small tomatoes, skinned
½ lettuce
2.5 ml spoon (½ level tsp) chopped
  basil
2.5 ml spoon (½ level tsp) chopped
  chervil
5 × 5 ml spoons (1½ tbsps) French
  dressing

Slice the white part of the leeks
very finely. Cut the tomatoes into
sections. Wash and drain the lettuce. Put the lettuce, leeks and
tomatoes into a salad bowl and
sprinkle on the basil and chervil.
Pour the dressing over the salad
and toss well before serving.

Orange salad

serves 4

2 oranges, peeled
chopped tarragon or mint

French dressing
endive or crisp lettuce leaves,
  washed

Divide the oranges into segments, removing all the skin, pith
and pips. Alternatively, cut across
in thin slices, using a saw-edged
knife.
Put the oranges into a shallow
dish, sprinkle with tarragon or
mint and pour the dressing over;
allow to stand for a short time.
Spoon the orange on to a bed of
endive or lettuce to serve.

Mushroom salad

serves 4

100 g (4 oz) mushrooms
10 ml spoon (2 tsps) lemon juice or
  cider vinegar
2 × 15 ml spoons (2 tbsps) salad oil
10 ml spoon (2 tsps) finely chopped
  parsley
freshly ground black pepper
salt

Wash and dry the mushrooms,
but do not peel; remove the stalks.
Slice the mushrooms very thinly

Just one pretty way of serving Orange salad

into a serving dish and add the
lemon juice, oil, parsley and pepper. Marinate in the dressing for
at least ½ hour and salt lightly
just before serving.

Apple-tuna salad

serves 4

175 g (6 oz) can tuna
1 small green pepper, seeded and
  chopped
4 medium red-skinned apples

For cheese dressing:
100 g (4 oz) cottage cheese
juice of ½ lemon
salt and pepper

Drain and flake the tuna and mix
with the pepper. Wash the apples,
discard the core and scoop out the
inside of each, leaving a 0.5 cm
(¼ in) wall. Chop the scooped-out
apple and add to the tuna mixture.
Combine the cottage cheese,
lemon juice and seasoning and
sieve or blend until smooth and
creamy. Add 1–2 × 15 ml spoons
(1–2 tbsps) to the tuna mixture
and mix thoroughly. Pile into the

apple shells and chill. Serve the
rest of the dressing separately.

Cabbage salad

serves 4

½ small white cabbage
1 small onion, skinned and
  chopped
5 × 5 ml spoons (1½ tbsps) French
  dressing
2.5 ml spoon (½ level tsp) caraway
  seeds
½ × 2.5 ml spoon (¼ level tsp)
  dried marjoram

Trim cabbage, remove the outer
leaves, then wash and shred it.
Place it in a bowl and pour boiling water over it. After 10
minutes, drain and rinse under
cold running water to cool. Drain
the cabbage well and transfer it to
a salad bowl. Add the onion.
Make the French dressing,
adding the caraway seeds and
marjoram, and pour over.

Endive and tomato salad

serves 6

1 endive (or a Webb's lettuce)
3 tomatoes, skinned and quartered
bunch of watercress, washed and
  trimmed
½ a small onion, skinned and
  chopped

For dressing:
15 ml spoon (1 tbsp) lemon juice
2 × 15 ml spoons (2 tbsps) salad oil
salt and freshly ground black
  pepper
a pinch of dry mustard
a pinch of sugar

Wash and roughly break up the
endive or lettuce. Toss together
the salad ingredients in a large
bowl. Whisk together the ingredients for the dressing and spoon
over the salad. Toss until the
salad is evenly coated.

Right: *Leek and tomato salad and
Mushroom salad*

Pork and bean salad

serves 4

2 × 15 ml spoons (2 tbsps)
  chopped parsley
1 small onion, skinned and very
  finely chopped
5 ml spoon (1 level tsp) dry
  mustard
5 ml spoon (1 level tsp) French
  mustard
5 ml spoon (1 level tsp) paprika
5 ml spoon (1 level tsp) salt
freshly ground black pepper
½ × 2.5 ml spoon (¼ level tsp)
  grated nutmeg
10 ml spoon (2 level tsps) caster
  sugar
juice of 1 orange
4 × 15 ml spoons (4 tbsps) salad
  oil
2 × 15 ml spoons (2 tbsps)
  tarragon vinegar
200 g (7 oz) can red kidney beans,
  drained
2 large cooked potatoes, peeled and
  diced
½ kg (1 lb) cold, cooked pork
  sausages
2 eating apples, cored and diced
2 tomatoes, skinned and seeded

Put the parsley, onion, seasonings, spices, sugar, orange juice, oil and vinegar in a lidded container, close and shake to make a dressing. In a bowl, lightly toss together the beans, potatoes, sausages (cut into 0.5 cm (¼ in) slices) apples and chopped tomatoes. Fold the dressing through and leave to marinate for 30 minutes, giving the mixture an occasional stir. Turn into salad bowl for serving.

Jellied beetroot and apple salad

serves 6

1 pkt. red jelly
300 ml (½ pint) boiling water
150 ml (¼ pint) vinegar
2 × 15 ml spoons (2 tbsps) lemon
  juice

Stuffed pepper salad is served in slices, garnished with sprigs of watercress

½ kg (1 lb) cooked beetroot
2 eating apples
50 g (2 oz) shelled walnuts

Break up the jelly tablet, place it in a basin and dissolve it in the boiling water.
When dissolved, mix together the vinegar and lemon juice, make up to 300 ml (½ pint) with cold water and add to the hot jelly liquid. Peel and slice or dice the cooked beetroot; peel, core and slice the apples. Place the walnuts in the base of a 1.1 litre (2 pint) ring mould and add the beetroot and apple in layers.
Pour on the liquid jelly and leave in a cool place to set. To serve, unmould on to a flat plate and garnish.

Tomato and onion salad

serves 6

Skin and slice 6 tomatoes and arrange in a dish. Sprinkle with finely chopped onion, season and pour over 2 × 15 ml spoons (2 tbsps) French dressing. Sprinkle with chopped parsley and marjoram.

Beetroot and chicory salad

serves 4

3 heads chicory
4 × 15 ml spoons (4 tbsps)
  mayonnaise
5 ml spoon (1 tsp) lemon juice
grated rind of ½ orange
100 g (4 oz) cooked beetroot
15 ml spoon (1 tbsp) oil
2 × 15 ml spoons (2 tbsps) vinegar
salt and freshly ground black
  pepper
½ × 2.5 ml spoon (¼ level tsp)
  French mustard

Discard a thin slice from the base of the chicory, discard any damaged outer leaves. Finely shred the chicory. In a bowl combine with the mayonnaise and lemon juice. Divide between 4 small plates and sprinkle with grated orange rind. Cut the beetroot into small, thin sticks and pile a little in the centre of each plate.
In a small tightly-lidded container combine the oil, vinegar, salt, black pepper and mustard. Spoon this over the beetroot and serve at once.
If wished, prepare the chicory mayonnaise and dress the beetroot with the oil and vinegar dressing a little time ahead. Keep in separate bowls and combine just before serving.

Stuffed pepper salad

serves 4

1 small red and 1 small green
  pepper
40 g (1½ oz) cottage cheese
40 g (1½ oz) cream cheese
chives, chopped
1 very small onion, skinned and
  chopped
salt and pepper
parsley, chopped
watercress

Cut away a thin slice from the stem end of each pepper. Wash and remove seeds. Beat together the cottage cheese, cream cheese, chopped chives and chopped onion, seasoning and parsley. Stuff the seasoned cheese mixture into the peppers, press firmly and chill for about ½ hour.
To serve, slice the peppers and arrange in rows. Garnish with watercress sprigs.

Piquant egg salad with yoghurt dressing – mix as near serving as possible for crisp, fresh-tasting vegetables

Hot potato salad

serves 4

4 rashers streaky bacon
1 small onion, skinned and diced
15 ml spoon (1 level tbsp) flour
15 ml spoon (1 tbsp) sugar
5 ml spoon (1 level tsp) salt
2.5 ml spoon (½ level tsp) paprika
6 × 15 ml spoons (6 tbsps) cider vinegar
7 × 15 ml spoons (7 tbsps) water
2 eggs, hard-boiled
4 cooked potatoes (about ½ kg (1 lb))
chopped parsley

Rind the bacon and snip it into 1 cm (½ in) pieces. Fry slowly until the fat runs, then add the onion and cook until golden. Stir in the flour, sugar, salt, paprika, vinegar and water. Cook for about 2 minutes, stirring. Add the sliced eggs and cubed potatoes. Heat for about 10 minutes, stirring occasionally. Garnish with parsley when serving. This salad is good for supper with cold roast pork.

Courgette and rice salad

serves 6

4 courgettes
100 g (4 oz) long grain rice
2 tomatoes
8 black olives
French dressing
fresh mint
10 ml spoon (2 tsps) chopped fresh basil

Slice the courgettes, discarding a thin slice from the top and bottom, and cook (without peeling) in boiling salted water until just tender but still crisp. Drain well. Boil the rice, drain and allow to dry a little. Slice the tomatoes; stone and halve the olives. Mix the courgettes and olives with the rice, toss in the dressing and pile into a dish; surround with tomato slices. Spoon a little more dressing over the tomatoes and garnish with herbs.

Piquant egg salad with yoghurt dressing

serves 4

For dressing:
300 ml (½ pint) low-fat natural yoghurt
5 ml spoon (1 level tsp) paprika
5 ml spoon (1 level tsp) sugar
15 ml spoon (1 tbsp) lemon juice
15 ml spoon (1 tbsp) orange juice
pepper
15 ml spoon (1 tbsp) finely chopped parsley

For the salad:
1 head celery, scrubbed and finely sliced
4 eggs, hard-boiled and sliced
4 carrots, peeled and grated
a few radishes, washed and sliced
½ cucumber (or 1 small ridge cucumber)

For the dressing combine the natural yoghurt with the paprika, sugar, strained lemon and orange juices, a little pepper and the finely chopped parsley.

Fold the celery through half the dressing and spoon into a salad bowl. Arrange the eggs on top, cover with the grated carrot and surround with sliced radishes and cucumber.

Spoon the remaining yoghurt dressing over the top. Chill before serving.

Smoked roe salad

serves 4

1 lemon
150 ml (¼ pint) mayonnaise
few drops Tabasco sauce
salt and freshly ground black pepper
4 slices white bread from a medium-sliced white loaf
butter
1 small lettuce
3 large eggs, hard-boiled
225 g (½ lb) smoked cods' roe
paprika

Blend the juice from ½ the lemon into the mayonnaise, add a few drops of Tabasco and adjust the seasoning.

Toast the bread until golden brown on both sides. Cool a little and butter liberally whilst still crisp. Lay 3 or 4 lettuce leaves on each slice of toast and spoon the mayonnaise down the centre. Slice the eggs and position overlapping down one side of the toast. Slice the roe and position down the opposite side. Take 4 slices from the remaining ½ lemon, make a cut into the centre of each slice, twist and place on top. Dust the egg with paprika and serve.

Mexican bean appetizer

serves 6

425 g (15 oz) can red kidney beans
4 sticks celery, chopped
25 g (1 oz) gherkins, chopped
2 × 15 ml spoons (2 level tbsps)
* finely chopped onion*
4 × 15 ml spoons (4 tbsps) oil
2 × 15 ml spoons (2 tbsps) malt
* vinegar*
2.5 ml spoon (½ level tsp) French
* mustard*
½ × 2.5 ml spoon (¼ level tsp)
* caster sugar*
salt and freshly ground black
* pepper*
2 eggs, hard-boiled
1 cos lettuce heart
a few celery leaves (optional)

Drain the kidney beans well and combine in a bowl with the chopped celery, chopped gherkins and onion. In a tightly-lidded container, place the oil, vinegar, mustard, sugar, salt and pepper. Shake well and pour over the bean mixture and fold through. Slice the eggs lengthwise. Arrange 2 lettuce leaves on each plate. Pile the bean mixture on to the base of these, spooning over any remaining dressing. Place 3 slices of hard-boiled egg on each and add a few celery leaves either side.

Right: *serve Mexican bean appetizer on a bed of fresh lettuce*

Eggs & Cheese

basic ingredients turned into something special

Chakchouka

serves 4

25 g (1 oz) lard
½ kg (1 lb) tomatoes, skinned and
  sliced
350 g (¾ lb) potatoes, peeled and
  sliced
100 g (4 oz) green peppers, seeded
  and finely chopped
1 clove garlic, skinned and crushed
salt and freshly ground black
  pepper
4 eggs

Melt the lard in a saucepan and
fry the tomatoes and potatoes
slowly for 20 minutes. Add the
peppers and garlic, season and
simmer for a further 15 minutes.
Poach the eggs in gently simmering water for 3–4 minutes. Turn
the vegetables into a hot serving
dish, drain the eggs and arrange
them on top of the vegetables.

Cheese omelette

serves 1

2 eggs
salt and pepper
15 g (½ oz) butter or margarine
50 g (2 oz) cheese, grated

Break the eggs into a basin and
beat lightly with a fork. Add
2 × 15 ml spoons (2 tbsps) water
and some salt and pepper and mix
well. Melt the butter in a frying
pan over a medium heat.
Pour in the beaten egg and stir
gently with the back of a fork (or a
wooden spatula if you are using a
non-stick pan).
Draw the sides of the omelette in
to the centre of the pan, so that the
liquid egg can flow to the sides
and so cook.
When the eggs start to set, stop
stirring and leave the pan until
the omelette is set and the underside golden brown. Sprinkle the
grated cheese over the top. Turn
one side of the omelette in
towards the centre, then fold over
the opposite side to meet it.
Tip the omelette out on to a hot
plate so that the folded sides are
underneath and serve at once.

Eggs fritura

serves 4

1 green pepper, seeded and
  blanched
50 g (2 oz) butter
½ an onion, skinned and chopped
4 tomatoes, skinned and chopped
salt and freshly ground black
  pepper
4 eggs
4 rounds of toast
butter
50 g (2 oz) Cheddar cheese, grated
parsley to garnish

Chop the pepper, melt the butter
in a frying pan and fry the pepper
and onion. Add the tomatoes,
plenty of salt and pepper and cook
for 15 minutes.
Meanwhile poach the eggs.
Spoon the vegetable mixture on
to the buttered toast and place a
poached egg on each portion.
Sprinkle with grated cheese and
grill quickly.
Garnish with parsley.

Hot stuffed eggs

serves 4

4 eggs, hard-boiled
40 g (1½ oz) margarine
50 g (2 oz) mushrooms, wiped and
  chopped
1 onion, skinned and chopped

Probably the simplest and best of omelettes – Cheese omelette

Red house soufflé – a melt-in-the-mouth supper dish or first course

300 ml (½ pint) can tomato juice
5 ml spoon (1 level tsp) sugar
salt and pepper
10 ml spoon (2 level tsps) cornflour

Cut the eggs in half lengthwise and remove the yolks. Melt the margarine in a pan and lightly fry the mushrooms and onion in the hot fat for 5 minutes until golden brown. Put half the mixture in a basin. To the remaining mixture in the pan, add the tomato juice, sugar and seasoning; cook for 5 minutes. Blend the cornflour to a smooth cream with a little water. Stir in a little of the hot tomato juice and return it to the pan. Bring to the boil, stirring until it thickens, and continue cooking for 1–2 minutes. Keep this sauce hot. Meanwhile, mix the egg yolks with the onion and mushroom mixture in the basin and use to stuff the egg halves. Arrange the halves in a dish and pour the sauce over.

Red house soufflé

serves 6

50 g (2 oz) butter
225 g (8 oz) onions, skinned and thinly sliced
100 g (4 oz) frozen sweetcorn
225 g (8 oz) tomatoes, skinned and thickly sliced
2 × 15 ml spoons (2 tbsps) chopped parsley

For the sauce:
50 g (2 oz) butter
50 g (2 oz) flour
600 ml (1 pint) milk
salt and freshly ground black pepper
175 g (6 oz) strong Cheddar cheese, grated
6 eggs, separated

Butter a 2 litre (3½ pint) soufflé dish or casserole. Heat 50 g (2 oz) butter in a frying pan, add the onion and sauté until soft but not coloured. Add the corn and continue cooking for 5 minutes. Remove from the heat and add the tomatoes and parsley.

For the sauce, melt 50 g (2 oz) butter in a saucepan, stir in the flour and cook for a few minutes. Gradually add the milk, stirring all the time, bring to the boil and simmer for a few minutes.

Add half the sauce to the vegetables and check the seasoning. Turn the mixture into the soufflé dish or casserole.

Add the cheese to the remaining sauce in the pan, beat in the egg yolks and adjust the seasoning again. Stiffly whisk the egg whites and fold into the sauce with a metal spoon.

Spoon the mixture over the vegetables and bake in the centre of oven for about 1 hour at 180°C (350°F) mark 4 until well risen and golden. Serve at once.

Cheese soufflé

serves 4

40 g (1½ oz) butter
4 large eggs
25 g (1 oz) plain flour
300 ml (½ pint) milk
175 g (6 oz) dry Cheddar cheese, finely grated
salt and pepper

Butter a 1.1 litre (2 pint) capacity soufflé dish. Separate the eggs. Melt the butter, stir in the flour and cook for 2–3 minutes.

Gradually stir in the milk, beating the mixure until smooth. Cook for a few minutes longer. Add the egg yolks one at a time, beating well, stir in the cheese and season. Stiffly whisk the egg whites, fold these quickly and evenly into the cheese mixture with a metal spoon and turn into the soufflé dish.

Bake in the centre of the oven at 180°C (350°F) mark 4 for about 45 minutes until well risen and brown. Serve immediately.

Bacon and onion soufflé

serves 4

25 g (1 oz) butter
175 g (6 oz) lean bacon, rinded and
chopped
225 g (8 oz) onion, skinned and
chopped
15 ml spoon (1 tbsp) chopped
parsley
salt and pepper

For the sauce:
50 g (2 oz) butter
40 g (1½ oz) plain flour
300 ml (½ pint) milk
3 egg yolks
4 egg whites

Butter a 1.4 litre (2½ pint) capacity soufflé dish. Melt 25 g (1 oz) butter in a medium pan, add the bacon and fry for 2–3 minutes. Add the onion and continue cooking until the onion is tender. Remove from the heat. Add the parsley and season to taste. Melt the 50 g (2 oz) butter in a saucepan, add the flour and stir well with a wooden spoon. Cook for 2–3 minutes. Add the milk gradually and bring to the boil, stirring continuously. Mix half the sauce with half the bacon and onion mixture and spoon into the soufflé dish.

Beat the egg yolks one at a time into the remaining sauce. Whisk the egg whites until stiff and gently fold, with a metal spoon, into the sauce. Add the remaining bacon mixture. Turn into the soufflé dish, bake near the top of the oven at 190°C (375°F) mark 5 for about 45 minutes until well risen and golden.
Serve at once.

Cauliflower au gratin

serves 4

1 kg (2 lb) potatoes
2 large eggs, beaten separately
salt and pepper
40 g (1½ oz) butter
1 kg (2 lb) cauliflower
300 ml (½ pint) can condensed
cream of celery soup
2 × 15 ml spoons (2 tbsps) milk
100 g (4 oz) well-flavoured
Cheddar cheese
50 g (2 oz) buttered crumbs

Peel potatoes and cook in boiling salted water. Drain and sieve back into the pan, then beat in 2 × 15 ml spoons (2 tbsps) beaten egg, butter and seasoning. With a large nozzle, pipe the potato round the edge of a shallow gratin dish, brush with the remainder of the first egg. Brown in the oven at 200°C (400°F) mark 6 for about 20 minutes, or under the grill. Meanwhile, break the cauliflower into sprigs and cook in boiling salted water until tender but not mushy. Drain well and arrange in the centre of the potato.

In a saucepan, whisk together the soup, the second egg, milk and cheese. Bring to simmering point, stirring, and then pour over the cauliflower. Top with the buttered crumbs and return to the oven or grill to reheat.

Corn and cheese omelette

serves 2

4 eggs
2 × 15 ml spoons (2 tbsps) water
salt and freshly ground black
pepper
25 g (1 oz) butter
200 g (7 oz) can sweet corn with
peppers
50 g (2 oz) Lancashire cheese,
grated

To make an omelette for 1 person, beat 2 eggs lightly with 15 ml spoon (1 tbsp) water. Season to taste. Heat half the butter in a heavy-bottomed frying pan, tilting the pan to grease the whole surface, and pour in the egg mixture. Stir gently with the back of a fork, from the sides towards the centre, until no liquid egg remains. Stop stirring and cook a little longer to lightly brown the omelette underneath. Meanwhile, heat the sweet corn in a separate pan.

When the egg mixture has almost set, spread half the corn down the centre and towards one side. Sprinkle with 25 g (1 oz) grated cheese. Tilt the pan and let the omelette fold over.

Keep hot while you repeat for the second omelette. Serve the omelettes at once.

Garnish Curried scramble with onion, parsley and tomatoes

Curried scramble

serves 2

1 small onion, skinned and
chopped
fat for frying
3 × 2.5 ml spoons (1½ level tsps)
curry powder
4 eggs
5 ml spoon (1 tsp) chopped parsley
15 ml spoon (1 tbsp) milk
salt and freshly ground black
pepper
2 large slices buttered toast or 4
crumpets

Fry the onion in a little fat until soft but not coloured, then add the curry powder and fry slowly for 5 minutes.

Beat together the eggs, parsley, milk and seasoning. Add to the pan and cook gently, stirring constantly and lifting the egg from the bottom of the pan.

Serve on hot buttered toast or toasted crumpets.

Scrambled egg nests

serves 4

4 × 15 ml spoons (4 tbsps) mashed
potatoes
flour
bacon fat or dripping
2–3 eggs
salt and freshly ground black
pepper
a little milk
a knob of butter
watercress or parsley for garnish

Shape the mashed potato into 4 flat cakes and flour them lightly. Fry in the bacon fat or dripping until golden brown on the underside. Turn the cakes over and hollow the centre of each slightly with the bowl of a spoon. Leave over a gentle heat to brown underneath.

Meanwhile, beat the eggs lightly with salt and pepper, add the milk and cook very slowly in hot butter, stirring gently until lightly set.

Fill the centres of the potato

Spaghetti con formaggio is generously covered in melted cheese

cakes with the scrambled egg and garnish with watercress or parsley.

Spaghetti con formaggio

serves 4

275 g (10 oz) spaghetti
½ kg (1 lb) lean streaky bacon, rinded and chopped
100 g (4 oz) onion, skinned and coarsely grated
50 g (2 oz) butter
¼ kg (½ lb) button mushrooms, sliced
salt and freshly ground black pepper
2 × 15 ml spoons (2 tbsps) salad oil
350 g (12 oz) mature Cheddar cheese, grated
chopped parsley

Cook the spaghetti in boiling salted water for 10 minutes. Put the chopped bacon in a frying pan and fry gently for 3 minutes, stirring occasionally with a wooden spoon. Add the onion and cook for a further 1 minute. Add the butter and sliced mushrooms, season lightly and cook for 4 minutes, stirring occasionally. Drain the pasta and return it to the pan with the salad oil. Using 2 forks, coat the spaghetti in the oil until it glistens. Light the grill.

Turn the spaghetti into a flameproof dish and spoon the bacon and mushroom mixture on top. Sprinkle with grated cheese and grill under a fierce heat for about 30 seconds. Sprinkle with chopped parsley before serving.

Marrow soufflé

serves 4

½ kg (1 lb) marrow, peeled
50 g (2 oz) butter
25 g (1 oz) plain flour
300 ml (½ pint) milk
salt and freshly ground black pepper
10 ml spoon (2 level tsps) dried summer savory
3 eggs, separated
100 g (4 oz) cheese, grated

Butter a 1.1 litre (2 pint) capacity soufflé dish. Cut the marrow into thick slices and discard the seeds. Cook in boiling, salted water until tender but still firm. Drain well and roughly chop. Put into a bowl and set aside.
Melt the butter and stir in the flour. Gradually stir in the milk and seasoning. Pour half this sauce over the marrow, add the herbs and spoon into the soufflé dish.
Beat the egg yolks and add to the remaining sauce, with the cheese. Adjust seasoning. Stiffly whisk the egg whites and fold in. Spoon over the marrow.
Bake in the oven at 190°C (375°F) mark 5 for about 30 minutes, until well risen.
Serve at once.

Eggs en cocotte

serves 4

2 rashers of bacon, chopped
4 eggs
salt and freshly ground black pepper
butter

Divide the bacon between 4 ramekins or individual soufflé dishes and bake towards the top of the oven at 180°C (350°F) mark 4 for about 8 minutes, or until the bacon pieces are lightly cooked (not brown).
Break an egg into each dish, sprinkle with salt and pepper. Put a few dots of butter on each and bake just above the centre of the oven for 7–10 minutes until the eggs are lightly set.
Serve hot.

Jacket potatoes with curried egg filling

serves 6

6 even-sized, large potatoes
cooking oil

For curried egg filling:
2 eggs, hard-boiled and shelled
15 g (½ oz) butter
50 g (2 oz) onion, skinned and chopped
2.5 ml spoon (½ level tsp) curry powder
50 g (2 oz) cooking apple, peeled and diced
salt and freshly ground black pepper

Wash, scrub and dry the potatoes. Prick with a fork and brush with oil, then place on a baking sheet and cook in the oven at 180°C (350°F) mark 4 for about 1½ hours.
For the filling, sieve one egg, fry the onion in the butter until soft but not coloured; add the curry powder and apple and fry for a further 5 minutes, then add the sieved egg. Cut lids from the tops of the potatoes when they are cooked and scoop out the centres, leaving a wall of skin. Mix the soft potato with the curried mixture and season well. Replace the mixture inside the potato shells and garnish with the remaining egg, sliced.
Serve with mango chutney.

Double-crust bacon and egg pie

serves 4

175 g (6 oz) plain flour
2.5 ml spoon (½ level tsp) salt
75 g (3 oz) lard or half lard and half margarine
about 3 × 10 ml spoons (6 tsps) cold water
175 g (6 oz) streaky bacon, rinded
2 eggs
2 × 15 ml spoons (2 tbsps) milk
salt and pepper
extra milk to glaze the pastry

Sift the flour and salt into a mixing bowl. Add the fat, cut up in small pieces and rub into the flour with cool fingertips until the mixture resembles breadcrumbs.
Sprinkle the water over the mixture. Mix with a round-bladed knife until the dough sticks together. Using one hand, knead it lightly into a smooth, firm ball. Cut the bacon into small pieces using a pair of scissors. Break the eggs into a basin, whisk lightly and then stir in the milk, salt and pepper.
Divide the dough equally into 2 pieces and roll out 1 piece on a lightly floured surface into a round a little bigger than an 18 cm (7 in) pie plate. Carefully lift the pastry on to the plate. Put the bacon on the pastry and pour the egg mixture over it. Roll out the remaining pastry to fit the top of the plate and put in position. Press the edges together all round. Trim any excess pastry.

Eggs à la florentine is a classic dish

Then hold down the edges of the pastry with the back of your forefinger and make horizontal cuts along the edge, then push in the edges every 2.5 cm (1 in) or so to make a scallop. Brush with milk.

Put the pie on a baking tray and bake near the top of the oven at 200°C (400°F) mark 6 for 30 minutes.

Spanish omelette

serves 2

butter or oil for frying
1 small onion, skinned and chopped
2–3 mushrooms, wiped and sliced
1 cooked potato, diced
225 g (8 oz) canned pimiento, chopped
small quantity cooked peas, beans or carrots
4 eggs
salt and freshly ground black pepper
chopped parsley

Put enough butter or oil in a 20.5 cm (8 in) frying pan just to cover the base.
Add the onion and sauté until soft but not coloured. Add the mushrooms and cook until tender. Add the potato, pimiento and cooked vegetables. Heat thoroughly.
Lightly mix the eggs, season and pour over the vegetable mixture, which should be bubbling. When just set, turn upside down on to a heated serving dish. Garnish with chopped parsley and serve at once.

Eggs à la florentine

serves 4

½ kg (1 lb) spinach
salt and pepper
40 g (1½ oz) butter
25 g (1 oz) plain flour
300 ml (½ pint) milk
65 g (2½ oz) Parmesan or Cheddar cheese, grated
4 eggs
3 × 15 ml spoons (3 tbsps) single cream
tomato slices to garnish

Wash the spinach well, put it into a pan with a little salt and just the water that clings to the leaves. Cook for 10–15 minutes, until tender.
Meanwhile make a cheese sauce. Melt 25 g (1 oz) butter in a pan, blend in the flour and cook over a gentle heat for 1 minute. Remove pan from heat, stir in milk and bring to the boil, stirring. Cook for 2 minutes. Stir in 50 g (2 oz) of grated cheese. Drain spinach well, chop roughly, mix with 15 g (½ oz) butter and season. Put into an ovenproof dish. Poach the eggs lightly and place side by side on the spinach. Pour cheese sauce and cream over eggs and sprinkle with remaining cheese. Put dish in the centre of the oven set at 190°C (375°F) mark 5 and bake for 10–15 minutes, until golden. Alternatively, brown under the grill. Garnish with tomato slices.

Oeufs maison

serves 2·4

100 g (4 oz) frozen peas
1 onion, skinned and finely chopped
4 tomatoes, skinned and chopped
2.5 ml spoon (½ level tsp) garlic salt
salt and freshly ground black pepper
3 large eggs
300 ml (½ pint) milk
parsley

Cook the peas according to the directions on the packet. Just before the end of the cooking time, add the chopped onion and blanch for 1–2 minutes. Drain. Divide the peas, onion and tomatoes between 4 individual ovenproof soup bowls or soufflé dishes. Sprinkle the salts and pepper over the top. Place the eggs and milk in a bowl, beat with a fork to mix then strain over the vegetables. Place the dishes in a roasting tin with water to come half way up, and cook in the oven at 190°C (375°F) mark 5 for about 40 minutes. Garnish with parsley and serve with crusty bread.

Raised bacon and egg pie

serves 8

For hot water crust:
450 g (1 lb) plain flour
10 ml spoon (2 level tsps) salt
100 g (4 oz) lard
200 ml (7 fl oz) milk or water
beaten egg to glaze

For filling:
1 kg (2 lb) bacon joint, cooked
1 egg, lightly beaten
2 × 15 ml spoons (2 level tbsps) tomato paste
3 × 15 ml spoons (3 tbsps) chopped parsley
freshly ground black pepper
3 eggs, hard-boiled
300 ml (½ pint) aspic jelly, made from aspic jelly powder

Sift the flour and salt into a basin and put in a warm place. Melt the lard and add the liquid. Bring to the boil and pour the mixture into the flour. Mix to a paste quickly, using a wooden spoon, turn it on to a floured board and knead until the dough is smooth and free from cracks. Cut off a quarter of the dough and put aside. Use the rest to line an 18 cm (7 in) round cake tin; take care to keep the pastry warm whilst moulding.
Divide the cooked bacon joint in half. Mince one half and mix the meat with the beaten egg, tomato paste, parsley and pepper to make a forcemeat. Chop and mix the remaining bacon and 2 of the cooked eggs.
Line the pastry with the forcemeat. Fill the centre with the chopped bacon and eggs, placing the remaining hard-boiled egg in the centre.
Roll out the remaining piece of pastry to make a lid. Cover the pie and press the edges together to form a rim and scallop it. Make a

Use up leftover vegetables in a Spanish omelette

cut in the centre to allow steam to escape and decorate the pie with leaves cut from the pastry trimmings. Brush with beaten egg. Bake the pie in the centre of the oven at 220°C (425°F) mark 7 for 30 minutes. Reduce the temperature to 180°C (350°F) mark 4 and cook for a further 15 minutes. Carefully remove the pie from the tin and allow to cool.

Make up the aspic jelly and when it is on the point of setting, pour it into the pie through the hole in the centre of the lid. Chill to set the jelly completely.

Cauliflower fondue

serves 4

6 eggs
½ kg (1 lb) cauliflower florets
4 × 15 ml spoons (4 tbsps) milk
5 ml (1 level tsp) cornflour
few drops Worcestershire sauce
pinch salt and pepper
225 g (8 oz) Cheddar cheese, grated
2 × 15 ml spoons (2 tbsps) chopped parsley

Hard-boil two of the eggs. Cook the even-sized florets of cauliflower in salted water for about 10 minutes; they should be tender but still crisp. Drain.

While the cauliflower is cooking, combine the milk, cornflour, Worcester sauce and seasoning in the top of a double boiler. (If care is taken, a small pan can be used over a low heat). Heat until the cornflour thickens, then add cheese. When the cheese melts, stir in the remaining four eggs, previously beaten, and continue to stir until the sauce thickens. Arrange the cauliflower in four individual, pre-heated earthenware dishes; spoon the sauce over. Garnish with chopped hard-boiled egg mixed with parsley. Serve with toast fingers.

Stuffed rolls

serves 4

4 crisp dinner rolls
25 g (1 oz) butter

Stuffed rolls – a good way to use up any stale rolls

50 g (2 oz) mushrooms, wiped and sliced
3 tomatoes, skinned and chopped
1 small onion, skinned and grated
3 eggs
salt and pepper

Cut a slice from the top of each roll and scoop out some of the soft inside. Melt the butter, add the vegetables and fry for 5–10 minutes, until soft but not coloured. Whisk the eggs with some seasoning, pour into the pan and stir with a wooden spoon over a low heat until the mixture scrambles. Pile it into the bread shells, replace the lids and place on a baking sheet. Cook in the centre of the oven at 200°C (400°F) mark 6 for about 15 minutes, until the rolls are crisp and the filling thoroughly heated.

Butter bean quiche

serves 4

200 g (7 oz) shortcrust pastry (200 g (7 oz) flour etc.)
40 g (1½ oz) Cheddar cheese, grated
2 eggs
300 ml (½ pint) milk

425 g (15 oz) can butter beans, drained
salt and pepper
2.5 ml spoon (½ level tsp) dried basil
2 tomatoes, skinned and sliced

Roll out the pastry and use it to line a 21.5 cm (8½ in) flan ring. Sprinkle with three-quarters of the grated cheese. Beat the eggs lightly with the milk and add the butter beans. Season well with salt, pepper and basil. Pour the savoury custard over the cheese and arrange the slices of tomato on top. Sprinkle with the remaining cheese and bake at 200°C (400°F) mark 6 for 10 minutes. Reduce temperature to 180°C (350°F) mark 4 for a further 35 minutes. Serve with an apple and celery salad.

Ratatouille cheese pie

serves 4

375 g (13 oz) pkt of frozen puff pastry, thawed
175 g (6 oz) mature Cheddar cheese, grated
2 eggs, hard-boiled and quartered
425 g (15 oz) can ratatouille

grated rind of ½ lemon
15 ml spoon (1 tbsp) lemon juice
salt and freshly ground black pepper
15 ml spoon (1 tbsp) chopped chives
beaten egg

Roll out half the pastry into a 25.5 cm (10 in) round and place on a dampened baking sheet. Place cheese, eggs and ratatouille in layers on pastry. Season with lemon rind, juice, salt and pepper. Sprinkle with chives. Leave a 1 cm (½ in) rim round the pastry edge. Brush edge with egg.

Roll out the remaining pastry in a similar way to a slightly larger round and use as lid.

Press the edge lightly to seal and knock up with the back of a knife. Chill for 30 minutes. Brush pastry with beaten egg and make a slit in the lid.

Bake at 240°C (450°F) mark 8 for about 25 minutes until golden and puffed up. Eat warm or cold.

Onion and apple open tart

serves 4

½ kg (1 lb) cooking apples
1–2 onions, parboiled
100 g (4 oz) shortcrust pastry (100 g (4 oz) plain flour etc.)
100 g (4 oz) cheese, grated
2 eggs
300 ml (½ pint) milk
salt and pepper
tomatoes (optional)

Peel, core and slice the apples; chop the onions. Put the apples and onions into a pan with a very little water and simmer gently until tender. Line a pie-plate with the pastry, put in the cooled apple and onion mixture and sprinkle with the cheese. Beat the eggs and pour on the milk; season and pour over the filling. Bake towards the top of the oven at 220°C (425°F) mark 7 for 10 minutes to brown the pastry, then at 180°C (350°F) mark 4 for a further 20–30 minutes until the custard is set.

Slices of tomato may be placed over the top about halfway through the baking time. Serve either hot or cold.

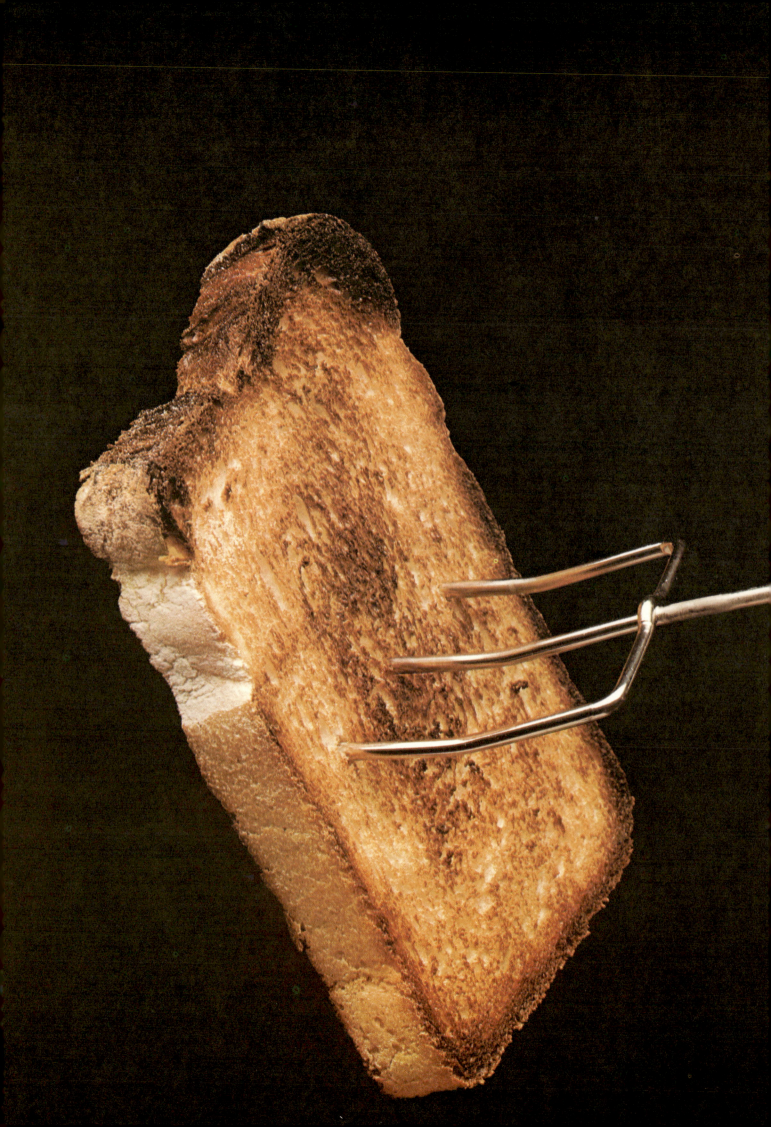

Snacks, Lunches & Suppers

the quick light meal

Egg and vegetable flan

serves 4

100 g (4 oz) shortcrust pastry i.e.
  made with 100 g (4 oz) flour etc.
25 g (1 oz) butter
25 g (1 oz) flour
300 ml (½ pint) milk
75 g (3 oz) cheese, grated
salt and pepper
3 eggs, hard-boiled and sliced
100 g (4 oz) frozen mixed
  vegetables

Roll out the pastry and use it to line an 18 cm (7 in) flan ring or case. Bake blind at 200°C (400°F) mark 6 until lightly browned. Cool. This can be done a day ahead.

Melt the butter, stir in the flour and cook for 2–3 minutes. Remove the pan from the heat and gradually stir in the milk. Bring to the boil and continue to cook, stirring, until the sauce thickens and is cooked. Stir in the cheese and season to taste. Arrange the sliced eggs in the cooled flan case, retaining 2–3 slices for garnishing. Cook the frozen vegetables according to the directions on the packet, mix them with the cheese sauce, cool a little and spoon into the flan case. Leave until cold. Garnish with the remaining slices of egg.

Pizza with gammon and onion

serves 6

For dough:
150 ml (¼ pint) water
7 g (¼ oz) fresh baker's yeast
225 g (8 oz) plain bread flour
5 ml spoon (1 level tsp) salt
7 g (¼ oz) lard
cooking oil

For filling:
½ kg (1 lb) gammon, rinded and
  cut into 0.5 cm (¼ in) cubes

3 × 15 ml spoons (3 tbsps) cooking
  oil
½ kg (1 lb) onions, skinned and
  sliced
10 ml spoon (2 level tsps) dried
  marjoram
salt and pepper
100 g (4 oz) Bel Paese cheese,
  grated

Grease a shallow rectangular tin measuring about 30.5 cm (12 in) by 21.5 cm (8½ in). Warm the water, sprinkle on the yeast and leave until frothy. Sift together the flour and salt, rub in the lard and stir in the yeast mixture. Knead, cover with oiled polythene and leave until doubled in size. Roll out dough on a lightly floured board to fit the base of the prepared tin. Brush with oil. Fry the gammon in oil until sealed. Remove from the pan and fry the onions lightly. Mix with the gammon. Spread the mixture over the dough and sprinkle with marjoram, salt and pepper, then cover with grated cheese. Bake in the centre of the oven at 230°C (450°F) mark 8 for 20 minutes, cover loosely with foil and continue to cook for another 20 minutes.

Green bean and bacon flan

serves 4

For cheese pastry:
100 g (4 oz) self-raising flour
a pinch of salt
50 g (2 oz) butter, margarine or
  lard
50 g (2 oz) Cheddar cheese, grated
a little beaten egg or water

For filling:
4 × 15 ml spoons (4 tbsps) milk
50 g (2 oz) cheese, grated
4 eggs, beaten
salt and pepper
4 rashers streaky bacon, rinded
100 g (4 oz) cooked green beans

Sift together the flour and salt and rub in the fat until the mixture resembles fine crumbs. Stir in the cheese. Bind together with enough egg or water to give a firm but pliable dough. Roll out and use to line a 20.5 cm (8 in) plain flan ring. Bake blind at 200°C (400°F) mark 6 for about 10 minutes. Remove from the oven and reduce the temperature to 190°C (375°F) mark 5. Stir together the milk, cheese and eggs and adjust seasoning. Grill or fry the bacon until crisp, then cut into small pieces. Arrange half the bacon in the flan case and pour on a little of the egg mixture. Add the beans and the rest of the bacon and coat with the rest of the egg. Bake for about 30 minutes or until just firm. Serve hot or cold.

Tomato and tuna en gelée

serves 4

300 ml (½ pint) tomato juice
3 × 2.5 ml spoons (1½ level tsps)
  powdered gelatine
2 × 200 g (2 × 7 oz) cans tuna
4 eggs, hard-boiled and sliced
lemon juice
salt and pepper
cress to garnish

Heat the tomato juice and sprinkle the gelatine over. When dissolved leave to cool. Flake the

Use frozen mixed vegetables for this tasty Egg and vegetable flan

tuna and add to the juice with 2 of the sliced hard-boiled eggs, a squeeze of lemon juice and plenty of seasoning. Pour into a 600 ml (1 pint) capacity ring mould and allow to set.

To serve, turn out of the mould, fill the centre with cress and surround with remaining hard-boiled eggs, chopped. Serve as a first course, or as a light lunch, accompanied by salad and crusty French bread.

Remove and chop the stalks from the mushrooms. Lightly fry the stalks and the onion in the butter for 2–5 minutes, until soft. Add the ham or bacon, breadcrumbs, cheese and parsley and enough egg to bind them all together. Stir until well mixed and hot, season to taste. Brush the mushrooms with a little oil and put in a greased baking tin. Pile the filling into the mushrooms, cover with greaseproof paper or foil and bake at 190°C (375°F) mark 5 for 20 minutes. Serve on toast.

Tomato and tuna en gelée – a first course or light lunch dish

Stuffed mushrooms on toast

serves 4

8 medium-sized mushrooms, wiped
15 g (½ oz) butter
1 small onion, skinned and finely chopped
3 × 15 ml spoons (3 tbsps) finely chopped cooked ham or bacon
5 × 15 ml spoons (5 level tbsps) fresh white breadcrumbs
25 g (1 oz) cheese, grated
5 ml spoon (1 tsp) chopped parsley
beaten egg to bind
salt and pepper
cooking oil
4 rounds of buttered toast

Pick of the pantry pizza

serves 4

15 ml spoon (1 level tbsp) dried onion flakes
boiling water
225 g (8 oz) self-raising flour
15 ml spoon (1 level tbsp) powdered stock
5 ml spoon (1 level tsp) baking powder
50 g (2 oz) butter or margarine
milk and water to mix
425 g (15 oz) can pilchards in tomato sauce
225 g (8 oz) can tomatoes, drained
75 g (3 oz) cheese, grated
freshly ground black pepper
chopped parsley (optional)

Soak the dried onion in boiling water for 5 minutes. Sift together the flour, powdered stock and baking powder.

Rub in the fat and mix to a firm scone dough with milk and water. Turn on to a floured board, knead lightly and roll to form a 23 cm (9 in) round or, better still, press into a 23 cm (9 in) flan ring. Drain the onions and spread over the dough. Arrange the pilchards on top with the drained tomatoes and sprinkle with cheese. Season with pepper.

Bake in the oven at 220°C (425°F) mark 7 for approximately 45 minutes. Cover with foil if necessary to prevent excessive browning. Serve hot from the oven, sprinkled with chopped parsley.

Slice the courgettes and cook in boiling salted water for 6 minutes; drain. Arrange all but a few slices of courgette and tomato in the base of a 2.3 litre (4 pint) flameproof dish. Dot with 25 g (1 oz) butter. Cover with foil and keep hot under a low grill.

Melt 100 g (4 oz) butter in a pan, add the onion and cook for about 2 minutes, until tender. Add the thyme and stir in the flour.

Remove the pan from the heat, blend in the milk, return to the heat and bring to the boil, stirring. Add the cheese and season well.

Melt the remaining 50 g (2 oz) butter in a frying pan and add the breadcrumbs.

Cook until well browned. Remove the foil from the vegetables, cover the cheese sauce and top with the crisp crumbs. Garnish with the remaining slices of courgette and tomato.

A dish for emergencies – Pick of the pantry pizza

Vegetable fricassée

serves 4

½ kg (1 lb) courgettes
½ kg (1 lb) firm tomatoes, skinned and sliced
200 g (7 oz) butter
¼ kg (½ lb) onions, skinned and sliced
5 ml spoon (1 level tsp) dried thyme
4 × 15 ml spoons (4 level tbsps) flour
900 ml (1½ pints) milk
¼ kg (½ lb) Cheddar cheese, grated
salt and pepper
100 g (4 oz) fresh brown breadcrumbs

Vegetable curry

serves 4

1 cauliflower, cut in large florets
6 tomatoes, skinned and sliced
8 small potatoes, peeled and quartered
100 g (4 oz) shelled peas
100 g (4 oz) French beans, sliced
15 ml spoon (1 level tbsp) turmeric
5 × 5 ml spoons (1½ level tbsp) mild curry powder
2.5 ml spoon (½ level tsp) salt
50 g (2 oz) butter

6 small onions, skinned
1 clove garlic, skinned and crushed
300 ml (½ pint) stock

Place the raw cauliflower, tomatoes, potatoes, peas and beans on a large plate. Mix the spices and salt and sprinkle over the vegetables. Melt the butter in a heavy pan and sauté the small onions and garlic. Add the spiced vegetables, then the stock; cover, bring to the boil and simmer for about 20 minutes, until all the vegetables are tender. Serve with boiled rice.

Bean and bacon sandwiches

serves 4

100 g (4 oz) can baked beans in tomato sauce
8 rashers streaky bacon, rinded
horseradish sauce
prepared mustard
8 slices white bread, from a ready-sliced loaf
butter

Heat the beans gently through in a small pan. Fry or grill the bacon until crisp, and then crumble on to a plate. When hot, mix the beans with a little horseradish sauce, to taste, and mustard, and stir in the crumbled bacon.
Toast the bread on both sides, butter and spread with the bean filling, as for an ordinary sandwich. Alternatively, butter the bread, untoasted, fill with the bean mixture and place each sandwich buttered side out in a special toasted sandwich cooker.

Beefeater pie

serves 6

pkt of beef stew seasoning mix
300 ml (½ pint) water
2 × 15 ml spoons (2 level tbsps) dried sliced onion
15 ml spoon (1 level tbsp) dried marjoram
2 × 350 g (2 × 12 oz) cans corned beef
2 × 450 g (2 × 16 oz) cans baked beans in tomato sauce

2 × 90 g (2 × 3½ oz) pkts instant mashed potato
50 g (2 oz) butter
salt and pepper
chopped chives

Mix together the seasoning and water in a saucepan until smooth. Add the onion and marjoram. Bring to the boil, then simmer. Cut the corned beef into 2.5 cm (1 in) cubes and add to the sauce, with the baked beans. Mix well, cover and simmer gently. Meanwhile make up the potatoes with water as directed on the packet. Beat butter and seasoning into the mashed potato. Turn the meat mixture into a casserole, spoon the potato over the top, fork up and brown under a hot grill. Sprinkle with chopped chives.

Hot stuffed tomatoes

serves 6

6 even-sized tomatoes
20 g (¾ oz) butter
40 g (1½ oz) ham, chopped
3 × 2.5 ml spoons (1½ tsps) chopped onion
5 ml spoon (1 tsp) chopped parsley
3 × 15 ml spoons (3 tbsps) fresh white breadcrumbs
salt and pepper
3 × 15 ml spoons (3 level tbsps) grated cheese (optional)

Cut a small round from each tomato at the end opposite the stalk, and scoop out the centres. Lightly fry the ham and onion in the butter for 3 minutes. Add the parsley, breadcrumbs, salt and pepper, cheese, if used, and the pulp removed from the tomatoes. Fill the tomato cases with this mixture, pile it neatly on top, put on the lids and bake at 200°C (400°F) mark 6 for about 15 minutes.

Cannelloni au gratin

serves 4

275 g (10 oz) cannelloni
a chunk of bread the size of an orange

milk
1 egg, hard-boiled and finely chopped
15 ml spoon (1 tbsp) chopped parsley
50 g (2 oz) mushrooms, chopped
salt and freshly ground black pepper
1 egg, beaten
a little single cream
300 ml (½ pint) béchamel sauce
50 g (2 oz) white breadcrumbs
grated Parmesan cheese

Cook the cannelloni in plenty of boiling, salted water for about 15 minutes and drain carefully.
Dip the bread into milk and squeeze then mash it. Add the hard-boiled egg, parsley and mushrooms. Season and add the raw egg and enough cream to moisten the mixture.
Carefully cut the cannelloni lengthwise, lay some stuffing along the centre of each and fold into their original form. Lay them in a well-buttered ovenproof dish, coat with the béchamel sauce, sprinkle them first with dry breadcrumbs and then grated Parmesan cheese and bake towards the top of the oven at 220°C (425°F) mark 7 for about 15 minutes.

Quiche lyonnaise

serves 4

100 g (4 oz) shortcrust pastry ie made with 100 g (4 oz) flour etc
2 × 15 ml spoons (2 tbsps) cooking oil
1 large onion, skinned and chopped
25 g (1 oz) butter
5 × 5 ml spoons (1½ level tbsps) flour
300 ml (½ pint) milk
100 g (4 oz) Cheddar cheese, grated
salt and freshly ground black pepper
4 eggs
parsley sprigs for garnish

Roll out the pastry and use to line a 20 cm (8 in) flan ring or tin. Bake blind in the oven at 200°C (400°F) mark 6 for 15 minutes. Fry the chopped onion in the oil until soft and evenly coloured. Drain off the fat and spread the onion over the base of the freshly

baked flan case. Melt the butter in a small pan, blend in the flour and cook for 2–3 minutes, without colouring. Blend in the milk and most of the cheese, reserving a little; bring to the boil, stirring and season. Keep this sauce warm. Poach the eggs in gently simmering water for 3–4 minutes. Drain well and arrange them on the onion, in the flan case. Coat with the cheese sauce, and sprinkle with the reserved grated cheese.
Place the flan under a pre-heated grill and brown quickly. Garnish with parsley sprigs and serve at once.

Quiche lorraine

serves 4-6

100 g (4 oz) frozen puff pastry, thawed
75–100 g (3–4 oz) lean bacon rashers, rinded and chopped
75–100 g (3–4 oz) Cheddar cheese, grated
2 eggs, beaten
150 ml (¼ pint) creamy milk
salt and pepper

Roll out the pastry thinly and line a 20.5 cm (8 in) plain flan ring or sandwich cake tin, making a double edge. Cover the bacon with boiling water and leave for 2–3 minutes, then drain well. Put into the pastry case with the cheese. Mix the eggs and milk, season well and pour into the case. Bake towards the top of the oven at 200°C (400°F) mark 6 for about 40 minutes until filling is set and pastry golden.

Lasagne

serves 4

2 × 400 g (2 × 14 oz) can tomatoes, drained
15 ml spoon (1 level tbsp) tomato paste
5 ml spoon (1 level tsp) dried marjoram
salt and freshly ground black pepper
½ kg (1 lb) lean minced beef
100 g (4 oz) lasagne strips
25 g (1 oz) butter
25 g (1 oz) flour

300 ml (½ pint) milk
175 g (6 oz) Cheddar cheese, grated
oil for glazing
100 g (4 oz) Mozzarella or Bel Paese cheese, sliced

Combine the canned tomatoes, tomato paste, marjoram, salt and pepper. Simmer in an open pan for 30 minutes. Add the beef and simmer for 25 minutes.

Cook the lasagne strips in a large pan of fast-boiling, salted water for 10–15 minutes and drain.

In a small saucepan, melt 25 g (1 oz) butter, stir in the flour and gradually blend in the milk. Bring to the boil, stirring constantly. Remove from the heat,

add the Cheddar cheese and season to taste.

Cover the base of an ovenproof dish (about 4 cm (1½ in) deep) with strips of lasagne. Add alternate layers of meat and cheese sauce. Finish the final layer with strips of pasta placed diagonally across, with the sauces spooned between. Lightly oil the pasta to prevent it drying.

Bake in the oven at 190°C (375°F) mark 5 for about 30 minutes. Remove from the oven, add the slices of Mozzarella on top of the cheese sauce. Raise the temperature to 220°C (425°F) mark 7 and return the lasagne to the oven until the cheese is golden and bubbling.

Cornish pasties

makes 4

350 g (12 oz) chuck, blade or skirt steak
100 g (4 oz) raw potato, peeled and diced
1 small onion, skinned and chopped
salt and pepper
350 g (12 oz) shortcrust pastry ie 350 g (12 oz) flour etc.

Cut the steak into small pieces, add the potato and onion and sea-

son well. Divide the pastry into four and roll each piece into a round about 20.5 cm (8 in) in diameter. Divide the meat mixture between the pastry rounds, damp the edges, draw the edges of the pastry together to form a seam across the top and flute the edges with the fingers.

Place on a baking tray and bake in the oven at 220°C (425°F) mark 7 for 15 minutes to start browning the pastry, then reduce the heat to 170°C (325°F) mark 3 and cook for about 1 hour. Serve hot or cold.

Serve this decorative Lasagne with green beans

Spaghetti alla bolognese

serves 4

1 onion, skinned and chopped
1 small carrot, peeled and chopped
1 celery stalk, scrubbed and
  chopped
1 clove garlic, skinned and crushed
2 × 15 ml spoons (2 tbsps) olive oil
25 g (1 oz) butter
1 bay leaf
150 ml (¼ pint) stock
350 g (12 oz) raw minced beef
425 g (15 oz) can tomatoes
2 × 15 ml spoons (2 level tbsps)
  tomato paste
meat extract
salt and pepper
350 g (12 oz) spaghetti
25 g (1 oz) butter
grated Parmesan cheese

Place the chopped onion, carrot, celery and garlic in a saucepan with the oil, butter and bay leaf. Fry for 5 minutes, then add the stock, meat, tomatoes and tomato paste, with meat extract and seasoning to taste. Cover and simmer for about 30 minutes. Remove bay leaf. Meanwhile cook the spaghetti in plenty of boiling salted water for about 20 minutes. Drain, toss in butter and sprinkle well with black pepper. Put into a hot serving dish and spoon the sauce over it; serve sprinkled with Parmesan cheese.

Stuffed French loaf

serves 4

1 small French loaf
5 celery stalks, scrubbed and
  chopped
a little butter
100 g (4 oz) cream cheese
2 × 15 ml spoons (2 tbsps) milk
salt and freshly ground black
  pepper

Cut a slice lengthways from the top of the loaf to make a lid. Set the lid aside.
Scoop out some of the inside to make room for the filling. Mix the celery, butter, cream cheese, milk

and seasoning and pile this filling into the loaf. Replace the lid. To serve, cut the loaf into 5–7.5 cm (2–3 in) slices.

Risotto alla piemontese

serves 4

225 g (8 oz) long grain rice
100 g (4 oz) lean bacon rashers,
  rinded and diced
900 ml (1½ pints) veal or chicken
  stock
5 ml spoon (1 level tsp) white
  pepper
150 ml (¼ pint) fresh tomato purée
  (see below)
15 ml spoon (1 tbsp) chopped onion
15 ml spoon (1 tbsp) chopped
  parsley
a few leaves of sweet basil
small cooked sausages

Put the rice in boiling salted water, bring back to the boil and boil for 5 minutes. Drain the rice and cool. Meanwhile, fry the diced bacon; when browned, put the stock and pepper in a large pan, add the bacon and the blanched rice. Simmer for 20 minutes, stirring occasionally. Remove from the heat, add the tomato purée, chopped onion, parsley and sweet basil. Reheat gently, stirring well. Pile on to a hot serving dish and surround with small cooked sausages.
To make 150 ml (¼ pint) fresh tomato purée, skin and chop 350 g (¾ lb) ripe tomatoes; place in a thick based pan, simmer gently until well reduced, then sieve.

Smoked haddock and cheese flan

serves 6

For flan case:
150 g (5 oz) plain flour
pinch of salt
75 g (3 oz) butter or margarine
1 egg yolk
2 × 10 ml spoons (4 tsps) water

For filling:
225 g (½ lb) smoked haddock

150 ml (¼ pint) water
juice of ½ lemon
25 g (1 oz) butter
1 small onion, skinned and finely
  chopped
50 g (2 oz) mushrooms, wiped and
  chopped
2 eggs
3 × 15 ml spoons (3 tbsps) single
  cream
100 g (4 oz) cottage cheese
salt and freshly ground black
  pepper
chopped parsley

Sift the flour and salt together. Cut the fat into small pieces and add to the flour. Rub the fat into the flour with the fingertips, until the mixture looks like fine breadcrumbs. Add the egg yolk, blended with 10 ml spoon (2 tsps) water; add more water if required to bind the dough. Knead lightly for a few seconds to give a firm, smooth dough. Put in a cool place to 'rest' for 15 minutes. Roll out the pastry to 0.3 cm (⅛ in) thick and use to line a 20.5 cm (8 in) flan ring. Prick the base of the case, line with foil and bake blind in the oven at 200°C (400°F) mark 6 for 15 minutes; remove foil and continue cooking for a further 5–10 minutes until the pastry is lightly browned. Cool. Poach the haddock in a pan with water and half the lemon juice. Drain the fish, discard the skin and bones and flake the flesh. Melt the butter in a pan, cook the onion for a few minutes then add the mushrooms and continue to cook for 3–4 minutes.
Combine the fish and vegetables and spread over the base of the flan case. Beat the eggs, add the cream, cheese and remaining lemon juice; adjust seasoning. Pour over the fish mixture. Bake in the oven at 190°C (375°F) mark 5 for about 35 minutes until set and golden. Garnish with chopped parsley. Serve hot or cold.

Trident toasted sandwiches

serves 4-6

2 large eggs, hard-boiled
100 g (4 oz) strong Cheddar
  cheese, grated
200 g (7 oz) can tuna steak,
  drained and flaked
5 sweet pickled onions, chopped
4 × 15 ml spoons (4 level tbsps)
  mayonnaise
juice of ½ lemon
few drops Tabasco sauce
salt and freshly ground black
  pepper
40 g (1½ oz) butter
12 slices from a large, white,
  medium-sliced loaf

Either chop the hard-boiled eggs or place in an egg slicer and cut in both directions. Combine the egg, cheese, tuna, pickled onions, mayonnaise, lemon juice, Tabasco, salt and pepper. Melt the butter in a small pan and brush it on to one side of each of the slices of bread. Place 6 of the slices, butter side down, on a board. Spread each with ⅙th of the filling, and top with another slice of bread, butter side up. Grill under a medium heat on both sides until golden. Cut in half and serve.

Tuna and spaghetti crisp

serves 4

100 g (4 oz) short-cut spaghetti

A huge Trident toasted sandwich will satisfy tea-time appetites

Bacon gnocchi is little squares made with semolina and cheese covering a delicious bacon mixture

200 g (7 oz) can tuna steak,
  drained and flaked
300 ml (½ pint) white sauce
75 g (3 oz) cheese, grated
salt and pepper
25 g (1 oz) pkt potato crisps

Cook the spaghetti in boiling salted water for 8–12 minutes. Drain well and place in a bowl. Add the drained and flaked tuna steak, the white sauce, cheese and seasoning. Mix well and transfer to a greased 1.1 litre (2 pint) casserole. Crush the crisps slightly and arrange on top. Bake for 20–30 minutes in the oven at 180°C (350°F) mark 4.

Vegetable samosas

serves 4

225 g (½ lb) potatoes, peeled and
  diced
225 g (½ lb) shelled green peas
salt and pepper
225 g (8 oz) self-raising flour
25 g (1 oz) butter or ghee
oil for deep-frying

Boil the potatoes with the peas; when cooked, drain and add salt and pepper to taste. Sift the flour and a pinch of salt into a bowl. Rub in the butter, add cold water and make into a pastry dough. Roll out 0.3 cm (⅛ in) thick and cut into 7.5 cm (3 in) rounds. Damp the edges.
Add 10 ml spoon (2 tsps) of the potato and pea mixture to each round of pastry, fold over into crescent shapes and seal the edges. Fry in hot oil until golden.

Barbecued sausages

serves 4

½ kg (1 lb) pork sausages
175 g (6 oz) pasta shapes
knob of butter
freshly ground black pepper

Sauce:
50 g (2 oz) butter
100 g (4 oz) onion, skinned
225 g (8 oz) can tomatoes
10 ml spoon (2 level tsps) tomato
  paste
2 × 15 ml spoons (2 tbsps) vinegar
2 × 15 ml spoons (2 level tbsps)
demerara sugar
10 ml spoon (2 level tsps) dry
  mustard
2 × 15 ml spoons (2 tbsps)
  Worcestershire sauce

Melt butter in a saucepan, add onion and cook gently until soft but not browned.
Stir in remaining ingredients except for the sausages and pasta. Simmer, partially covered, for 25 minutes.
Meanwhile grill or fry sausages until browned and cook pasta for 15 minutes in boiling water.
Drain pasta, add a knob of butter and milled black pepper and turn into a serving dish. Place sausages on pasta and cover with sauce.

Bacon gnocchi

serves 4-6

¾ kg (1½ lb) bacon hock joint
300 ml (½ pint) milk
50 g (2 oz) semolina
salt and black pepper
pinch of nutmeg
1 egg, beaten
2 × 15 ml spoons (2 level tbsps)
  Parmesan cheese
2 × 15 ml spoons (2 tbsps) corn oil
100 g (4 oz) onion, skinned and
  chopped
350 g (12 oz) can sweetcorn with
  peppers
75 g (3 oz) Cheddar cheese, grated
25 g (1 oz) butter, melted

Soak bacon for 2–3 hours.
Bring milk to the boil; when boiling shower in semolina and add seasonings. Cook, stirring until very thick. Off the heat, beat in the egg and cheese. Spread over a greased shallow tin to a depth of 1 cm (½ in) and leave to get cold. Discard skin and bone from bacon and cut into bite-size pieces. Fry gently in the oil for about 5 minutes. Add onion and cook a further 5 minutes. Off the heat stir in sweetcorn, with juice and season with black pepper. Turn bacon mixture into a 1.7 litre (3 pint) casserole dish layering the cheese between.
Cut gnocchi into 4 cm (1½ in) squares and place on top. Brush with melted butter and bake at 180°C (350°F) mark 4 for about 30 minutes. Raise temperature to 200°C (400°F) mark 6 for about a further 20 minutes.